INSTANT ANALYSIS

INSTANT ANALYSIS

Confessions of a White House Correspondent

FORREST BOYD

JOHN KNOX PRESS
ATLANTA, GEORGIA

Library of Congress Cataloging in Publication Data

Boyd, Forrest, 1921-
  Instant analysis--confessions of a White House correspondent.

  1. Journalism--Washington, D. C. 2. Presidents--
United States. 3. United States--Politics and govern-
ment--1945-   4. Boyd, Forrest, 1921-   I. Title.
PN4899.W29B6   172'.2   73-21356
ISBN 0-8042-0829-8

INSTANT ANALYSIS

CONTENTS

IT'S REALLY TRUE!

"Always tell the truth, but if you can't tell the truth, don't lie." That was said to be the motto of Bill Moyers when he was press secretary for President Lyndon B. Johnson. President Richard M. Nixon's press secretary, Ronald Ziegler, seemed to operate on another philosophy: "I know you believe you understood what you think I said, but I'm not sure you realize that what I said was not what I meant."

No wonder a reporter remarked at the beginning of a news briefing: "Speak up loudly and clearly, because the agnostics in this room are bad."

No wonder, during the Senate Watergate hearings, a perfect stranger commented to me as he picked up a paper at the newsstand, "I'm not sure I believe anybody."

During the hearings, too, the *Washington Star-News* editorialized that most TV viewers must have felt, "Well, somebody had to be telling the truth." The paper also quoted a U. S. district judge in another case: "Somebody had to believe in somebody."

During the 1960's and 1970's, there developed the credibility gap, or the crisis of confidence—a loss of confidence in almost everything, from political institutions, to the press, to our churches and all authority. A national polling group said it had found that 20 percent of the public did not believe that man ever made it to the moon. Neil Armstrong's climbing down the ladder and taking that "giant leap for mankind" was a colossal illusion, a put-on to make the world believe the Americans had done what, in fact, neither they, nor the Russians, nor anyone else, had accomplished. With a similar conclusion, comedian Mark Russell entertained at our White House correspondents dinner soon after one of the men-on-the-moon missions. Three astronauts who had just returned from the moon were sitting at the head table. Russell said he didn't believe they had been to the moon. He observed that when one of them reported that he was surveying an area that looked like a vast wasteland, "How do we know he wasn't in Baltimore?"

That typifies the skepticism of our day. During my coverage of the administrations of Lyndon B. Johnson and Richard M. Nixon, there has been an unusual preoccupation of the public with truth. With LBJ, we were obsessed with the credibility gap that seemed to grow out of the Vietnam war and official explanations of it. With Nixon, it was Watergate and the unprecedented public Senate hearings that were carried live by radio and television. People who had heard witness after witness purporting to be telling the truth began to talk and think in double positives. They would say, "This is really the truth." Or, "Honestly." Press secretary Ronald Ziegler once used a significant phrase in a briefing of the White House press at the Surf and Sand Hotel in Laguna Beach, California: "And that has the added virtue of being the truth." We could only conclude that what he had been saying at other times did not have that virtue. Conversations during this period underscored the value of Dr. Francis A. Schaeffer's precise reference to "true truth."

One of the more intriguing portions of the Watergate hearings was one in which the chairman, Sam Ervin, was putting questions to Gerald Alch, former attorney for convicted Watergate conspirator James McCord. Ervin was puzzling over how to determine which man was telling the truth, McCord or Alch. Alch suggested a polygraph test. Senator Ervin immediately put a damper on that, contending he was trying to conduct the hearings along legal lines and to keep to the kind of evidence that would stand up in court. He said lie detector tests are not accepted in court testimony. They were nothing but twentieth-century witchcraft, he said. At that point, Senator Howard Baker, the vice chairman, spoke up. Contrary to being twentieth-century witchcraft, he said, polygraph tests were very useful and are widely used by attorneys. Senator Baker contended that no one should be forced to take the tests, but if they wanted to the committee should let them. Then he proposed an alternative: Let both sides take the tests before the committee counsel, and then decide whether to reveal the results to the committee. Senator Ervin had a brief consultation with Samuel Dash, the committee's majority counsel, and without even recognizing that he had heard Senator Baker resumed his questioning of Alch. Nothing more was said about it in the hearings. Newsmen got to McCord and his new attorney, Bernard Fensterwald, who said they'd both be willing to take the lie detector tests, provided all witnesses did the same. They didn't. But Philadelphia Mayor Frank L. Rizzo did take a lie detector test sometime after that to clear himself of newspaper charges and flunked it. What made it particularly embarrassing was that before taking the test he said, "I have great confidence in the polygraph. If this machine said a man lied, he lied."

So far, the polygraph has not been the answer to our credibility problem. If it were, we can imagine everyone's being supplied with a small portable machine to take along when he buys a car, when he asks a friend about his golf score, or when he questions the veracity of public officials.

We now realize that a sense of confidence in our leaders and in each other is of vital importance. Our society begins to break down if there is a crisis of confidence, and there is a domino effect, in that one occasion of deceit influences another. In our city, for example, we were told by the service manager of the garage where our car was being repaired that checks would not be accepted, only cash. The reason was that many customers had discovered while driving their just-repaired cars home that the problems hadn't been fixed, so they would stop payment on the checks.

Before some department stores will accept a check for more than a certain amount, they demand all kinds of references and an on-the-spot photograph.

Before accepting credit cards, some hotel cashiers thumb through a large book of delinquent credit card holders.

There are several meanings to the word "truth." There is truth as fact. There is truth in the sense of honesty. And I think there is a third meaning: truth in the sense of an absolute, in which case we talk about seeking truth, or what is true.

There is another distinction I would like to make at this point: the relation of credibility to truth. There was a lot of talk during the Watergate hearings about the credibility of witnesses. I was often asked who I thought was most credible when there was conflicting testimony. I believe the questions were misguided sometimes because they implied credibility and truth were the same.

What do we mean by credibility? First, it is believability. A person can appear to be telling the truth and maintain almost total credibility even though he may be telling lies. Credibility is the ability to convince people one is telling the truth. It has to do with a listener's perception of what is the truth. It could be that the individual who is the best liar would have the greatest credibility, at least for a while. And the person who happens to look tricky or even ill at ease, or who is not a convincing speaker, could tell the truth so as not to be believable. The person who lies the most could be the most credible because he has had the most practice. Other things affect credibility, too. I noticed that during the Watergate hearings people had different reasons for thinking one witness or the other was credible. A boyish face. The amount of details given. A certain amount of confession. A proper mixture of truth with untruth. A confident manner.

The attitude of the listener is a factor, too. If a listener is gullible, the speaker is easily credible. If a listener is extremely skeptical, nothing to him is believable. A skeptic once told me: "Intellectual skeptics are emotionally motivated and have huge blind spots where they refuse to see." I'm convinced that people listen with a bias. I have had letters in answer to my commentaries on the Mutual Broadcasting System in which I was soundly condemned for saying something I didn't say. The problem was that the listener heard a word or a phrase and put his interpretation on it, because he was convinced that all Eastern journalists are left-wing liberals. Liberals listened with a bias because they assumed I was pro-president since I tried to be fair to President Nixon.

One more credibility factor: I was reminded of it by a cartoon in a *New Yorker* magazine. It showed a creature that I assume was the devil, planting seeds in a garden. The label on the seed packet was "doubt." There was no caption on the cartoon, and I was rather glad of that, because I had some fun making my own captions and applying them to different circumstances. It is clear to me that an individual's credibility can be damaged very simply—just by anyone's dropping a hint of doubt. LBJ's credibility gap was greatly exaggerated by all the talk about it. Every time a columnist wrote about Johnson's credibility gap, he made it bigger. Just the use of the word "credibility" in connection with President Johnson created a credibility problem. Imagine your reaction if you are introduced by a friend to a stranger, and as the stranger is saying, "How do you do," your friend whispers to you, "Credibility." You don't have to know anything about the person, but you already have a credibility problem with him.

That, to me, is the "devil" planting doubts in the garden of your mind. That's something we must watch if we are to make fair judgments about the credibility of witnesses. We must ask if we are being influenced by the doubts planted in our minds.

We must also recognize the fact that sometimes the greatest truth is incredible. We might remember that the skeptics tested Jesus on this point. "If you are the Son of God, come down from the cross." The implication was that if Jesus did that, they would believe. He knew better. The truth was incredible. Truth is stranger than fiction. If Watergate had been the plot of a novel, nobody would have believed it could happen. The book reviewers would have panned it as too far out.

In a sense, credibility is believability credit that a person stores up. It is truth reputation. When someone asks us to believe him because he says so or tells us to take his word for it, he can expect us to do so only if he has established a record for truthfulness.

I think this is why Lyndon Johnson and Richard Nixon had their problems with credibility. Johnson came to the White House with a "wheeler-dealer" reputation. Nixon came as "tricky Dick." Thus, when either man asked the public to take his word for anything, his reputation loomed large in the background.

An example of the opposite was suggested when President Nixon made his compromise offer on White House tapes containing conversations that referred to Watergate. The president suggested that transcripts of the tapes be made available to the special prosecutor and that their accuracy be verified by someone with an impeccable reputation for integrity. The man he suggested was Senator John Stennis, the president arguing that Stennis' honesty was not questioned by anyone, Democrat or Republican. Later, explaining his resignation as attorney general, Elliot Richardson said Stennis was selected because he was a man who would have his toenails pulled out one by one before he would endorse anything but the truth. Stennis would be one man who could successfully ask someone to believe his word with no supporting evidence. I have wondered if it would have helped us all know the truth if Stennis had been appointed an official administration verifier.

Considering what has happened to us, what has brought us where we are, what has changed our life-styles, what has caused flip-flops in our philosophies, what has changed our values, and what has shaken our institutions and our top leaders, I think we would miss the point if we did not consider what has happened to our concept of truth and what is true.

As we analyze events of these turbulent years, we will see that truth is elusive, truth is painful, truth is liberating, truth is eternal.

THE RIGHT TO LIE

The Watergate grand jury decided that former presidential aide Egil Krogh did not have the right to lie to it, in the name of national security and indicted him on two charges of perjury. He had headed what was nicknamed the White House "plumbers" in the Nixon administration; his unit was established to plug the leaks of national security information. Krogh asked U. S. District Court Judge Gerhard A. Gesell for dismissal of the charges on the grounds that he had been ordered to preserve the secrecy of the plumbers' work, even if he had to perjure himself. The judge said "no way." Krogh later changed his mind and decided to cooperate with the prosecution. In the deal, the government dropped the perjury charges and Krogh pleaded guilty to a new charge of conspiracy to violate the civil rights of the psychiatrist of Daniel Ellsberg, a plumbers' target.

The Watergate case seemed to bring together a number of aspects of official lying. It was not the actual breaking into the Democratic headquarters at the Watergate office complex that was such a great sin. It was the cover-up that followed, the lying to protect those involved. One of the greatest blows to believability in Washington was delivered by President Nixon's press secretary, Ronald Ziegler, on April 17, 1973. That date and what Ziegler said will long be remembered as the day something dreadful happened to White House credibility.

Prior to that date, he and President Nixon had steadfastly insisted that no one on the White House staff, no one in the administration, was involved in what the president called

"this very bizarre incident." Clark MacGregor, the chief of
the Committee to Re-Elect the President, had said, "Using in-
nuendo, third-person hearsay, unsubstantiated charges, anony-
mous sources and huge scare headlines, the [*Washington*]
Post has maliciously sought to give the appearance of a direct connection between the White House and the Watergate,
a charge which the *Post* knows—and a half a dozen investigations have found—to be false." Deputy director of the
committee, Jeb Stuart Magruder, told a *Time* magazine correspondent: "Listen, when this is all over, you'll know that
there were only seven people who knew about the Watergate,
and they are the seven who were indicted by the grand jury."
Standing on the sidewalk in front of the Executive Office
Building next to the White House, Magruder told me much
the same thing. Senate Republican leader Hugh Scott had
quoted President Nixon as saying: "I have nothing to hide.
The White House has nothing to hide. I repeat, we have
nothing to hide, and you are authorized to make that statement in my name." Press secretary Ziegler had "flatly" denied "any prior knowledge on the part of John Dean regard-
ing Watergate." When the *Washington Post* had reported that
the White House chief of staff, H. R. Haldeman, was involved in the approval of payments from a secret Nixon campaign cash fund, Ziegler denounced the paper for engaging in
a "political effort" at "character assassination" that he said
was the "shoddiest type of journalism." He said, "I will say
that it is political and it is an effort to discredit individuals
within this Administration based on hearsay and it is a blatant effort at character assassination that I do not think has
been witnessed in the political process in some time." Ziegler
denied that Haldeman had access to a secret fund, and also
denied the existence of the fund itself.

Then came April 17, 4:42 p.m., Eastern standard time.
White House correspondents had been alerted to expect some-

thing, and were called into the briefing room. The president appeared with an announcement about executive privilege, and then:

"On March 21st, as a result of serious charges which came to my attention, some of which were publicly reported, I began intensive new inquiries into this whole matter.

"Last Sunday afternoon, the Attorney General, Assistant Attorney General Petersen and I met at length in the E.O.B. to review the facts which had come to me in my investigation and also to review the progress of the Department of Justice Investigation.

"I can report today that there have been major developments in the case concerning which it would be improper to be more specific now, except to say that real progress has been made in finding the truth.

"If any person in the executive branch or in the Government is indicted by the grand jury, my policy will be to immediately suspend him. If he is convicted, he will, of course, be automatically discharged.

"I have expressed to the appropriate authorities my view that no individual holding, in the past or at present, a position of major importance in the Administration should be given immunity from prosecution.

"The judicial process is moving ahead as it should; and I shall aid it in all appropriate ways and have so informed the appropriate authorities.

"As I have said before and I have said throughout this entire matter, all government employees and especially White House staff employees are expected fully to cooperate in this matter. I condemn any attempts to cover up in this case, no matter who is involved."

Later in the afternoon, Ronald Ziegler held a briefing, of which the following is a partial transcript:

QUESTION: Ron, is this statement still correct? On March

2, the president said that the investigation conducted by Mr. Dean indicates no one on the White House staff, at the time he conducted the investigation, was involved or had knowledge of the Watergate matter. Does that still stand?

ZIEGLER: Well, of course, that was a statement made prior to the president's statement and the president's statement today is the operative statement. And the comment that the president made at that time was based upon investigations prior to the president's action which is indicated in today's statement.

QUESTION: Ron, this morning, Jerry [deputy press secretary Gerald Warren], after extreme reluctance, affirmed that that statement was still White House policy. That was true at noon, but that no longer operates?

ZIEGLER: The statement that the president made this afternoon is the operative statement or the standing statement of position.

QUESTION: It doesn't refer to this, it doesn't contradict it in any way and it doesn't relate to it in any way?

ZIEGLER: I think I responded to your question by saying that the statement made at the time of the comment you refer to was based on investigations that took place prior to this statement or prior to the activity which the president has been involved in in the past few weeks. The statement which the president made at that time was based on the previous investigation. Because of the scope of the statement today, I have to respond to your question by saying that today's statement, this afternoon's statement, is the operative position.

Later, in the same briefing . . .

QUESTION: Ron, could I follow up on your comment about the operative statement? Would it be fair for us to infer since what the president said today is now considered the operative statement, to quote you, that the other statement is no longer operative, that it is now inoperative?

ZIEGLER: The other statements that were made were based on information that was provided prior to these events which have been referred to in the president's statement today. Therefore, any comment which was made up until today or previously was based on that activity. This is the operative statement. The way to assess the previous comments is to assess them on the basis that they were made on the information available at that time. The president refers to the fact that there is new material; therefore, this is the operative statement, the others are inoperative.

The import of Ziegler's admission was that what we had been told emphatically for months, day after day, was not true. If anyone wonders why the press is skeptical, ponder the fact that we had been misled for so long. After that day when we were told previous statements were inoperative, we would question every statement. Is this operative? How can we tell, just because you say so? Did you talk to the president? Did you verify it? Credibility was washed away by the implications of that one word: inoperative.

A couple of weeks later, the day after another presidential statement and a surprise appearance in the briefing room, Ziegler had another revealing briefing:

QUESTION: Ron, a question in view of the president's comments when he came out and said a few words to the press last evening. Are you ready to apologize to the *Washington Post* for your comments of last October?

ZIEGLER: I don't have the problem of the press giving me h--- because that happens on a relatively frequent basis. I think we would all have to say, and I would be, I think, remiss if I did not say that mistakes were made during this period in terms of comments that were made, perhaps. I would say that

I was overenthusiastic at that time in my comments about the *Post,* particularly if you look at it in the context of the developments that have taken place. A press secretary, in his job, has to attempt to reflect the presidency and the White House. He also finds himself speaking on his own from time to time, as I was doing on that occasion. It was an overstatement, I believe. In thinking about it at this point in time, yes, I would apologize to the *Post,* and I would apologize to Mr. [Robert] Woodward and Mr. [Carl] Bernstein [*Post* reporters]. Now, having said that, I don't want to say that I agree with everything they write, and everything they have written. I think that would be a mistake, too. But they have vigorously pursued this story and they deserve the credit and are receiving the credit for it. When we are wrong, we are wrong, and I would have to say I was in that case and other cases.

The feud with the *Washington Post* proved something about the Nixon administration's strategy of making the press the enemy. Not only did Ziegler castigate the *Post* for its Watergate reporting, but the administration waged a campaign of punishment against the paper. Officials fed stories to the *Post's* competitor, the *Star-News.* The *Post's* society reporter was excluded from the reporting "pools" that covered White House receptions. Traditional news sources were cut off. I strongly believe this made *Washington Post* editors and reporters angry enough to declare they would pursue the Watergate story to the end, even if it killed them. Conceivably, they might have stopped somewhere along the line had it not been for the treatment the White House was giving them. It shows the folly of the Nixon press policy. It may have had its temporary successes, but in that kind of fight with the press it's impossible to win.

On the credibility question, however, it has been my contention that once a spokesman tells a lie, his credibility from then and forever, is suspect. Even so, many government officials and spokesmen still believe that under certain circumstances the government has a right to lie or, at least, to tell something less than the truth.

The question came to the forefront during the Kennedy administration, when Arthur Sylvester, Pentagon spokesman, justified deliberate misinformation about the Cuban missile crisis. Sylvester had been asked a question about it at a Sigma Delta Chi meeting. He said, "It would seem to me basic, all through history, that a government's right—and by a government I mean a people, since in our country, in my judgment, the people express, have the right to express, and do express, every two and every four years what government they want—that it's inherent in that government's right, if necessary, to lie to save itself when it's going up into a nuclear war."

In subsequent testimony before a congressional committee on government information and policies, Sylvester explained that "any nation has the right of survival, self-preservation, particularly in this time when it can be faced almost overnight with a nuclear holocaust." He added, "I believe in times of extreme peril, it is incumbent upon the U. S. Government, through its chosen representatives, to protect the people it serves from destruction by the enemy." Sylvester tried to make the point that a government lie should be used in a very narrow context—only on rare occasions—at times "when the very survival of [the] country is at stake and where the spectre of nuclear holocaust is an imminent possibility . . . " That's when "it can become necessary to mislead the enemy by statements issued by public officials."

Dwight D. Eisenhower was quoted by Sylvester as having said, "In time of war or times of great crisis, you do use spies; you develop elaborate systems of deceit in order to confuse your enemy or your potential enemy. Now as long as you are doing something that for the moment looks almost necessary to keep your position, vis-a-vis your potential enemies, or your enemies, strong, and/or to improve it, then I think at least we ought to keep still and maybe even allow contrary stories to get out." Eisenhower cited one of the deceptive activities employed by him before D-day in the Second World War and concluded by saying, "So you don't just say that in such situations that the truth, the whole truth, must be instantly given, because it would be terrible. So, I think there has got to be the rule of reason. What is good for the United States of America? That really must be the rule we must apply to every one of these things."

Eisenhower, thus, uncovered several aspects of truth: you can say nothing and permit your listener to believe an untruth, you don't have to tell the whole truth, and there may be some higher virtue than truth.

A correspondent reported that when Sylvester went to Saigon to discuss information problems with reporters and the question of credibility of American officials was raised, he answered: "Look, if you think any American official is going to tell you the truth, then you're stupid. Did you hear that? —stupid!"

Years later, Bruce Herschensohn, a member of the White House staff under Richard Nixon, said he believed there were "crisis situations" when it would be advisable for the government to give "not completely accurate" information to the American people. He emphasized he was speaking as a private citizen.

These opinions have some merit, but the problem was expressed by publisher Gene Robb to the same congressional committee that heard Sylvester: "A government can successfully lie no more than once to its people. Thereafter everything it says and does becomes suspect. All the more so when a high-ranking government officer makes speeches to justify these lies."

There are various justifications for official lies. When former Vice-President Spiro T. Agnew was visiting the Indochina area, there was speculation he would visit Phnom Penh, the capital of Cambodia. At that time, Phnom Penh was not the safest place in the world. He consistently denied he would make the visit. But reporters traveling with him were notified one morning to be on the plane at a certain time and, surely enough, they flew to Phnom Penh. In flight, Agnew explained that he could not have admitted he planned to go to Phnom Penh because this advance notice to Communist insurgents could have endangered not only his life but the lives of the correspondents as well. I think this admission of having lied, no matter how good the reason, hurt Agnew's believability thereafter. When he stoutly insisted at a later time that he would never resign, I had some doubts. Thus, when he did a complete reversal and did resign, I was not too surprised.

I can understand some of the rationale behind misleading statements. During the Johnson administration, the question of antiballistic missile systems was raised in a White House briefing. It had been reported that the Soviets were deploying the missile defense system around Moscow, and possibly elsewhere. President Johnson was faced with the decision of whether to enter into the expensive race or try to persuade the Russians to agree to limit deployment of ABM's. A reporter asked the press secretary, George Christian: "George, have we started such a system, and if so where," Christian looked around the room, saw a correspondent for Tass, the official Soviet news agency, along with the other correspondents with pencil poised to write down the kind of information intelligence agents would dearly like to have. Such genuine security problems as this one are understandable. There are times when none of us can ask the president's spokesman to be absolutely candid.

There was a period of several days during the 1967 Middle East crisis when Christian held two separate briefings—the regular one with all correspondents present and another one for the smaller group of American regulars. He explained that he would like to answer some of our questions but hesitated to do so in the larger briefings because, he said, "I don't know half those people, and I can't give you background or off-the-record information with reporters there, including foreigners, who should not have it, and who are not familiar with our methods."

One of the penalties of an open society with a free press is that government spokesmen must at times so carefully word their statements that they are meaningless. Otherwise, all the efforts made behind the scenes by our diplomats could be undermined.

Official spokesmen have to be very careful because the world watches sometimes for even one significant word. I interviewed Chester Bowles for Mutual's "Capitol Assignment" one time. Bowles was then a Kennedy administration foreign affairs expert, and one of my questions concerned border fighting between China and India. The day after our interview was broadcast, Chinese officials were disputing his views, charging an imperialistic, aggressive, anti-Chinese attitude. I assumed the program was monitored in China either from a rebroadcast of it on Armed Forces Radio or from the Voice of America, which occasionally used our interviews. The point is, with such high-speed communications there is never a time for a casual, frivolous statement on international matters. Consequently, officials and their spokesmen sometimes avoid revealing certain information.

Akin to government lying is government secrecy. The *Miami Herald* once headed an editorial: "Lesson in government: to conceal is to lie." In other words, to hide the truth is as bad as telling what is not the truth. One is negative, the other positive. The editorial quoted the Sigma Delta Chi Freedom of Information Committee which condemned the Agriculture Department in the Johnson administration for covering up unsanitary conditions, endangering health, in non-federally inspected meat packing and poultry plants.

When the Nixon administration took over Washington, it claimed it would be an "open administration." I always wondered what that meant. I could never see that it meant any more access to government information nor any fewer restrictions on reporters. I don't know what the average citizen thinks Washington reporters can do. At the White House, for example, we're very limited. If we have a question about an action the president might take or how he might feel about a certain issue, we can't march into his office and ask him. White House guards and Secret Service agents would stop us before we even got near. Hardly any newsman can see the president by appointment, and if he could, the appointment would come days or weeks after he asked for it.

You can't even walk in and ask the press secretary. You have to make an appointment to see him. Usually the highest you can get quickly is an assistant or deputy press secretary, and when you see him, often he does not have the answer. White House correspondents are limited to a very small area of the west wing of the White House, and we can't go anywhere outside the press area without an escort and without having gotten clearance beforehand.

It wasn't always so. This story may explain the present condition: Once upon a time, the press could go from the west wing to the cafeteria in the Executive Office Building without clearance. The EOB is across West Executive Avenue from the White House but still within the White House complex. In it are many of the top aides and the best sources.

During the Johnson administration, steel company and union negotiators had been called to the White House to settle a labor dispute. Those were the days of "jawboning." President Johnson put them in a suite of rooms in the Executive Office Building and told them to stay until they reached agreement. Reporters, on the pretext of going over to the cafeteria, tried to get information on how the talks were going. One enterprising fellow wandered upstairs and talked to some of the negotiators who were taking a break outside the meeting room. When the White House people found out about it, they cut off the cafeteria privileges and the EOB was ruled off limits to reporters. Later, the president's chief of staff, Marvin Watson, was said to be considering building a wall between the White House and the Executive Office Building so we couldn't even see the EOB. Although it was never constructed, we often referred to "Watson's wall," and the very idea became a symbol of the secrecy of the Johnson administration. Nixon's "open" administration did nothing to change all of this. If anything, it clamped down tighter. Every evening in government offices, secretaries still locked file drawers and secured them with a steel rod; they affixed a red card that read "secret." My personal opinion is that Richard Nixon's obsession with secrecy was partly responsible for his troubles. When you declare you will tolerate no leaks of information, people will try harder to get it. Thus we had the leak and publication of the Pentagon Papers and the National Security Council notes that were known as the Anderson Papers. Several memos were leaked to the press. The president's reaction was to create a special unit in the White House to try to find the leaks. The drastic method of tapping telephones was used. And the celebrated activity was the burglary of the office of Daniel Ellsberg's psychiatrist.

Government spokesmen and officials use all sorts of devices to hide the truth. One is to pretend to answer a question without saying anything. Every Washington official learns this technique. It is the art of saying nothing. It begins with the premise that one must never give a simple "yes" or "no" answer to anything. That would be too clear. Just before he left the Johnson administration, McGeorge Bundy briefed us and, in answer to a question, rambled on for a considerable time. When he got through, he said something like this: "There, that's the longest nonanswer I've ever given." He said he had just mastered the art at the time he was leaving government.

We had a Capitol Hill correspondent at Mutual Broadcasting, named Richard Rendell, who got disgusted with nonanswers. One time during an interview, he asked a question of a congressman and then said, "Answer me yes, no, or I don't know."

Once at a White House briefing on domestic matters, presidential counselor Daniel Patrick Moynihan answered one final question as he ducked out the door to go to another meeting: "Yes, no, maybe."

There is a technique of including equivocations so that a spokesman can always come back when challenged and say that he had included a "might" or a "could." A correspondent observed that if one goes down, he should always go down with his equivocations flying. Always use a qualifying word or two. Don't ever say a certain thing will be done at a certain time. Say it "might" happen "sometime." Old-time State Department correspondents tell me that former Secretary of State John Foster Dulles was a master at this "fine print" technique. When reporters thought they had caught him in a lie, he would tell them to go back and very carefully check exactly what he said. Sure enough, there was usually a qualifying word or two that technically saved his credibility. Correspondents got so conditioned to this that if Dulles said, "This is Wednesday," they checked the calendar to make sure.

This is also known as ambiguity. Often statements or answers are purposely made ambiguous so that they could mean different things to different people. As a practical matter, such statements usually don't mean anything to anybody, they only serve the purpose of a spokesman who wishes to hide the facts.

Former State Department spokesman Robert McCloskey illustrated the point once when he told State Department correspondents: "For the sake of clarity, that ambiguity ought to remain."

Henry Kissinger had a word he used in a joking way: obtuseness. He said that when he taught at Harvard, obtuseness was considered the same as profundity. But in the White House press corps, we called in "fuzzing" an answer—phrasing in such a way as to cause reporters to wonder what it meant. President Nixon's much-quoted statement is: "I want to make one thing perfectly clear." But we found that not many things were perfectly clear. And press secretary Ziegler's expertise seemed to be in making things unclear. We often wondered, after hearing the answer, whether he understood the question.

I can understand the inclination of public officials to hide the truth, to be devious in answers, and even to lie, but I have to conclude it is shortsighted to do so. It might buy some time in a particular circumstance, but eventually the truth will catch up, and then the price of credibility will be paid.

I think the ideal would be to require officials to tell the truth in unmistakable language without equivocation and ambiguity. A public spokesman should be so well trained in communicating that he articulates the truth clearly in a way that the listener or reporter cannot possibly fail to understand and cannot misinterpret.

An interesting comment on this matter of truth was contained in a novel written by an East German, Stefan Heym, called *The King David Report*. In the novel, one of King Solomon's scribes advised on the method of writing a history of the reign of King David, Solomon's father. The scribe thinks up three ways to deal with undesirable facts in writing the history: (1) tell it all; (2) tell it with discretion; and (3) don't tell it. He decides on the second course because "discretion was truth controlled by wisdom."

Perhaps that is the answer, but however the truth is told, the public official should always be sure it is in a way that preserves his believability. We have learned that a loss of believability can have terrible consequences.

FORGIVE US OUR PRESS PASSES

Thomas Jefferson would have been proud of Richard Nixon when Nixon attacked the press. Nixon expressed his dislike for the press almost as well as Jefferson did. Jefferson was bitter about the press. To Thomas McKean, Jefferson said, "Even the best informed of the people have learnt that nothing in a newspaper is to be believed." To William A. Burwell, he said of newspapers, "They never utter truth." To John Nowell, he said, "To your request of my opinion of the manner in which a newspaper should be conducted, so as to be most useful, I should answer: 'By restraining it to true facts and sound principles only.' " He added, "I really look with commiseration over the great body of my fellow citizens, who, reading newspapers, live and die in the belief that they have known something of what has been passing in the world in their time. General facts may indeed be collected from them, such as that Europe is now at war, that Bonaparte has been a successful warrior . . . but no details can be relied on. I will add, that the man who never looks into a newspaper is better informed than he who reads them, inasmuch as he who knows nothing is nearer the truth than he whose mind is filled with falsehood and errors." And for Agnew-style rhetoric, Jefferson was not outdone: "I deplore, with you, the putrid state into which our newspapers have passed, and the malignity, the vulgarity and the mendacious spirit of those who write for them, and I enclose you a recent sample. These ordures are rapidly depraving the public taste and lessening its relish for sound food. As vehicles of information and a curb on our functionaries, they have rendered themselves useless, by forfeiting all title to belief."

While Jefferson is one of the most quoted early Americans on the press, it is interesting to note that our first president, George Washington, had his battles with the press. Jefferson reported on a violent outburst from President Washington at a cabinet meeting. It was precipitated when General Knox mentioned a recent newspaper lampoon of Washington. Jefferson said, "The president was much inflamed, got into one of those passions when he cannot command himself, ran on much on the personal abuse which had been bestowed on him, defied any man on earth to produce one single act of his since he had been in the government which was not done on the purest motives, that he had never repented but once the having slipped the moment of resigning his office, and that was every moment since, that . . . By God . . . he had rather be in his grave than in his present situation. That he had rather be on his farm than to be made emperor of the world and yet they were charging him with wanting to be king. That that Rascal Freneau . . . a newspaper editor . . . sent him three of his papers every day, as if he thought he would become the distributor of his papers, that he could see in this nothing but an impudent design to insult him . . . "

These quotes illustrate the historic antagonism between presidents and the press; recent presidents and vice presidents are not peculiar in their dislike for the press. It was not surprising at all that John F. Kennedy had some reporters transferred out of the White House and cancelled White House subscriptions to the *New York Herald Tribune.* Nor was it surprising that Lyndon B. Johnson often publicly scolded the press. Nor that Vice-President Spiro Agnew asked the Midwest Regional Republican Committee in Des Moines, Iowa, November 13, 1969, whether a form of censorship "exists when the news that 40 million Americans receive each night is determined by a handful of men responsible only to their corporate employers and is filtered through a handful of commentators who admit to their own set of biases."

Nor should it have been considered unusual when Richard Nixon took note of the "electronic media" in an October 26, 1973, press conference, saying he had never, in all of his 27 years of public life, heard such outrageous, vicious, distorted reporting.

Almost universally, the reaction of the press to all of the criticism over the years has been defensive. Seldom do you hear any acknowledgment from the press that any of the criticism is justified. But, here, at least, one reporter will "confess."

I think I should make clear, first, that the sins I'm concerned most about are not the type that at one time were conjured up about newspaper reporters as a bunch of hard-living, two-fisted drunks, although some alcohol has been mixed into a few stories. There was the time we sat in the press plane at Andrews Air Force Base waiting for Lyndon Johnson to make up his mind to leave the White House. The longer we waited, of course, the more the guys drank, until somebody remarked that if a match were lit the plane would blow up from the ignited fumes. There was the newspaper reporter who fell off a wall while trying to watch a president and broke his arm, and his colleagues wrote his copy for days without the home office knowing. And there was another reporter who fell down the steps of the plane and wrote his stories during that visit to Texas from his bed, getting second-hand information from his fellow reporters. And there was the time some of the White House press corps got into a fight with local photographers in a press club bar and threw at least one photographer in the San Antonio River. But drinking is not the real problem of the press.

Here is a catalogue of what I consider the more important sins: One of the foremost causes of misleading news stories is the tradition of writing what the newspaper trade calls a "hard lead." It's the first sentence of a news story that is supposed to summarize the story in an eye-catching way. And it often amounts to the reporter's idea of what a government official meant to say, not what he said. Every writer tries to come up with a snappy, interesting lead that tells all the essential parts of the entire story in a concise way and whets the appetite of the reader or listener. After a major appearance or news conference by the president, there is always byplay among correspondents: "What's your lead?" or "What are you leading with?" When President Johnson held press conferences at the LBJ ranch in Texas, for example, most of the leads were decided on the bus from the ranch to the press center in Johnson City, about 15 miles away. No filing was permitted at the ranch, and nothing could be filed until reporters reached the Johnson City press center, where telephones and teletypes had been installed in an old store. It was an educational experience to ride that bus after a press conference and hear top reporters from the *New York Times, Washington Post, Chicago Tribune, Los Angeles Times,* the wire services, magazines and networks exchange ideas on the lead. Often humor was injected. A reporter would declare in a loud voice what he considered a clever parody of the president's views. Example: "President Johnson comma in a news conference at the LBJ ranch comma declared he was not good enough to be Lady Bird's husband comma and announced his intention to file for divorce." That would be a take-off on a statement LBJ may have made about his having married above his class.

But after a few of these "funnies" the talk would become more serious, and there would be a debate over whether the lead was that the president had announced sending a few thousand more troops to Vietnam, or that the budget would exceed $100 billion for the first time in history. This seems like an innocent enough bit of journalistic mechanics, but it is extremely important because the lead represents the reporter's opinion of what was most significant, as he boils it down to size and "sharpens it up" for interest, interpretation enters and sometimes can give exactly the opposite of the meaning intended by the president. What makes the lead more important is that many, if not most, readers read only the first paragraph or so of even major stories. My personal opinion is that the most powerful influence in the communications world is not the column, or the editorial, or the TV special, but the lead and the headline that tops it. This is not restricted to the newspapers. The five-minute radio newscasts are so constructed because of time limitations that the writer finds he must use essentially only leads. Consequently, many radio newscasts are just a collection of leads.

One night after a state dinner at the White House, President Johnson confided to me his concern over the lead. We were standing in the great hallway of the executive mansion and he was particularly disturbed about interpretations of the U. S. involvement in the Dominican Republic. He felt that many leads were misleading and that most Americans were getting the wrong idea of what was actually happening and what he was actually doing. I noticed that for a time afterward, Bill Moyers, in his briefings, tried to call attention to what he thought was the lead material. A time or two he actually said, in effect, "If you're looking for the lead, this is it. . . . "

But although he was conscious of the importance of the lead, Johnson sometimes contributed to the problem. I recall his calling reporters into his office late one afternoon for the specific purpose of explaining how he was trimming government expenditures, delaying contracts, and deferring actual allocations in order to cool off the economy. He had been unhappy with some news stories and wanted everyone to get it straight. During the discussion, someone asked what he estimated the defense part of the new budget would be. He tried to evade an answer but couldn't resist and said in an offhand way that it might be around $73 billion. Then the discussion reverted to the government expenditure explanation. I'm sure the president hoped the lead in the papers and on radio and TV newscasts would be about his efforts to cut government spending, but almost unanimously the reporters rushed to their typewriters and pecked out the lead: "President Johnson revealed tonight that next year's defense budget may soar to a record $73 billion."

Another mechanical factor that greatly influences opinion, sometimes in a distorted way, is what is called the "overnighter." This is a story that is written and filed at night in time to make the next day's papers and the morning newscasts. It may be a rewrite of the day's news, an updating of the news, a rundown of what is expected to take place the day the story is used, sheer speculation, or, at best, brand new information that is given out in advance for morning release. The overnighter is quite conspicuous when a president is at a residence away from Washington. It was often difficult to write an overnighter on President Nixon's trips because it was difficult to find out what he would be doing the next day. Reporters joked a good deal about all the overnighters reading: "President Nixon is working and relaxing at his home on Key Biscayne." If we could get the information, we would write something more specific: "President Nixon will announce later today his choice for attorney general." If White House officials didn't provide any information, reporters guessed about what the president was doing.

We were kept late at the White House one evening because there was an important meeting of congressmen of both parties with President Johnson. There had been a bombing pause in North Vietnam, and we had a good idea the meeting was about the resumption of bombing which would probably be ordered during the night. But after we had waited quite a long time, a press office spokesman came to tell us we could go home, there would be no report on the meeting, no announcement. A correspondent reminded the spokesman: "If we don't get something out of here tonight, there are going to be some wild overnighters." The spokesman revised his thinking, told us to wait, and apparently convinced the president to reveal something about the meeting because we did get a report and the overnighters reflected a more enlightened account of what had gone on at the White House.

The overnighter is one of the most difficult stories to write because as a rule, nothing much happens during the night and the writer has to use his ingenuity to "freshen up" an old story or "go out on a limb" about what the day ahead may bring. It's much the same problem that a writer for a Sunday paper has. Robert Fleming, who was deputy press secretary for Lyndon Johnson, related in a speech how a reporter had written a pre-Easter Sunday story out of San Antonio: "President Johnson is in a foul mood this Easter Sunday, apparent for all to see." Fleming observed: "Any of us in the business, and those not in the business, knows that anybody that has such a Sunday story chore has filed it somewhere along about 11:00, 12:00, or 1:00 o'clock on Saturday noon. This reporter proposes to project himself into something. He does it with a certain bravery—or perhaps recklessness—but for a flat-out statement, if he wanted to write, as he did, that the 'cold front which hit Texas almost exactly duplicates the gloom of uncertainty and apprehension that today hangs over the LBJ ranch.' The reporter saw this from 78 miles away. He has better eyes than I have. And stronger perception, too."

Directly related to the overnighter and weekender is another mechanical fact of a newsman's life that contributes to misleading stories. It is the enormous appetite for news. The news organizations feel they are obligated to fill so much time or so much space whether there is any news or not. This leads to pure fabrication of stories sometimes and playing unimportant stories way out of proportion in other cases. One of the best examples is the half-hour television newscast. It would be unthinkable to report 10 minutes of the important news and announce: "Well, ladies and gentlemen, that's all the news that's important enough to justify taking up your time, so we're going to run cartoons or symphony music for the remainder of the half hour." As for radio's hourly newscasts, one station owner told me that he thought most people listened to them merely to find out what had not happened —to be assured that the nuclear bomb wasn't on the way or that some other catastrophe was not happening. I'm sure this man would be happy if the networks would just ring a bell on the hour to indicate that everything is OK. But that won't happen. If it's a "dry" news day, the White House correspondent may be called upon to do a "think piece" about the president's health or the credibility gap; the State Department correspondent may be asked to fill two or three minutes with speculation about this or that world situation. Sometimes these speculative stories result in "call backs" for the rest of us. Our editors call and ask "Where's your story on the president's mood?" And if we say there's no story there, there's nothing to it, it's just some reporter's speculation, the editor may still say, "We need something, and everybody's talking about it, do something anyway." So, we end up doing a story, even if it's nothing more than saying that the original story wasn't true or that the White House has no comment. But every time we mention it, we blow it up in the view of the public. There have been some ridiculous stories that have received a fantastic amount of coverage just because of news organizations' appetite for copy. It's a built-in mechanical thing that nobody can ignore.

There's also the fact that some publishers and reporters have an ax to grind. For one reason or other, they start on a particular story with a viewpoint and seek to prove it. I think that during the Johnson administration and carrying over into the Nixon administration there developed what was called "advocacy reporting." It was associated with the civil rights drive and the antiwar movement but spread into other areas. Reporters felt it their obligation to help one cause or another, so they set out to bolster a point of view. I was once told by an employer that he would never hire a certain reporter because that reporter always found what he was looking for. He meant that the reporter started with a preconceived conclusion and always saw only the facts that would prove his conclusion. That employer is considered by many journalists now to be old-fashioned. One of the old tenets of journalism was objectivity, but objectivity has taken a beating in recent years. The sins of the press also include errors that creep in through interpretive reporting. Sometimes strange things are done with the truth in the news business. The presidents I have covered have expressed the preference for talking directly to the people through radio and television rather than giving a story to reporters and letting them write it. The reason is that the reporters sometimes, if not most times, put their own spin on the ball so that the result is not what the president intended. Many times I'm sure presidents have been angry and surprised when they have read what they said. Presidents' moods are often misinterpreted. When an aluminum company announced plans to raise its prices, a New York newspaper wrote that LBJ was "sputtering mad" about it because he was then jawboning with business and labor to hold the line on prices and wages in order to avoid inflation as a result of the Vietnam war. I doubt very much that such a judgmental description of a man's mood would hold up in court if it were to be offered as evidence of a man's intentions. Who can really judge if the President is sputtering mad or irked, particularly when the person making the judgment has not seen him?

A descriptive word is often inserted by a desk rewrite man to spice a story. It is a more interesting report if a witness stomps out of a room than if he walks out. One reporter told me that when a certain national news magazine likes a man, he "strides confidently," but if the magazine doesn't like him, he "ambles slowly." Such interpretive reporting can be a disservice. It can unnecessarily complicate the affairs of our officials. It can arouse suspicion that may not be warranted. It can injure reputations, destroy effectiveness, and certainly distort facts.

There was a good example of interpretive reporting when President Nixon spent a weekend in Florida in 1973. After answering questions of Associated Press managing editors at Disney World, the president rode in a motorcade to McCoy Air Force Base at Orlando for the flight back to Key Biscayne. While shaking hands and visiting briefly with the people who had turned out to see him, the president patted a man on the face. Two reporters from the reporting pool saw it and finally decided to put it in the pool report for the other White House correspondents. They debated on what word to use because it would make all the difference in the world whether they used "pat," "strike," or "slap." They finally settled on the word "slap," although they made it clear it was not a forceful slap. Another reporter wrote a story saying the president "soundly slapped" a man on the face. The White House reacted angrily because this all happened at a time when the president was trying desperately to restore confidence after the Watergate scandal and allegations that he was psychologically under pressure and emotionally unstable.

Despite the dangers, I believe interpretive reporting is not only desirable but necessary. The general public is not equipped to make reasonable conclusions on the meanings of individual news items. The average person does not have files of related information to bring into the picture for perspective. He cannot check with other reporters on other beats or talk with other sources for additional opinions. The value of a good reporter is that he can take a new piece of information and put it into a jigsaw puzzle made up of other pieces of information and produce a total picture of a certain subject. Take a simple announcement like this: "The Federal Reserve Board has decided to raise the rate it is going to charge banks for money, which will mean higher interest rates to a borrower." How many Americans would know all that is involved and that the president of the United States would be angered by it and release a formal statement a couple of days later deploring the action? How could most American voters remember that the chairman of the Federal Reserve Board had made a controversial speech, warning against inflationary trends and the dangers of depression, and that the president's Council of Economic Advisers had taken the opposite view? Who would be expected to tie in the controversy of tight money versus easy money? Who would know that the Federal Reserve Board chairman feared a runaway economy, while the president and his advisers feared a slowdown in the expansion? How would average citizens be able to dig up the fact that the board had split four to three on the decision and that a board member would soon retire, giving the president the opportunity to appoint a more liberal member and thus balance the voting more to his point of view? Putting all the pieces together, it made a significant and fascinating story, but only because reporters had the tools to get all the facts and to interpret the simple announcement in the light of those facts. The American people would be woefully uninformed if given only the raw news as it comes from its source. In most cases it would be meaningless.

The press is prone to mistakes, too, in the selection of news, and the balance of the news that is printed or broadcast. I believe this has upset presidents as much as anything.

The theme of Vice-President Spiro Agnew's criticism of the television news was that a small handful of people, an unelected elite, selected the news that most Americans would see.

Lyndon Johnson used to be irked by the proportion of news stories devoted to anti-Vietnam protests. Speaking to the national convention of the Junior Chamber of Commerce in Baltimore, June 27, 1967, he said: "During a week a short time ago, our newspapers, our TV programs, and our radio commentators, informed us fully about the protesters and the 'peace-niks' who invaded the Pentagon. They came there to stay—they walked over the tulips; they sat down on the steps; they slept in the halls. And after we had analyzed it all carefully and the reports had been fully given—sometimes dramatically, occasionally emotionally—the 'sleep-ins' numbered 12, a bare even dozen. And during that very same week, there were 10,000 young Americans who voluntarily—on their own—walked into the military enlistment centers directed by the Pentagon and volunteered their services and their lives for America. Let me repeat, there were over 10,000 first-term enlistments in one week. Unfortunately, a student carrying a sign, or a protester wearing a beard, or an attention-seeker burning a draft card in front of a camera can get more attention—and more billing—than all 10,000 of these volunteers."

Another factor contributing to our "sins" has been the emphasis on pictures. A foreign visitor being photographed by a horde of cameramen with a president said, "You don't have a democracy here, you have a photocracy." Eric Sevareid said the original trouble with TV was that its managers fell in love with the pictures and what didn't move wasn't news. Sevareid gave an example of an event in Vietnam. Buddhists staged some riots in Saigon and Da Nang. The TV cameras wheeled up. They focused of course on whatever was most dramatically in motion. He said the pictures could not show that a block away from the Saigon riots the populace was shopping, chatting, sitting in restaurants in total normalcy. The riots involved a tiny proportion of the people in either city; yet the effect of the pictures in this country, including in the Congress, was explosive. People here thought Vietnam was tearing itself apart and civil war was raging. Nothing of the sort was happening.

Part of the reason for the protest against the Vietnam war was that it was a picture war so far as American TV viewers were concerned. We got a distorted view because the cameras had to go where the action was. Naturally, there was much more coverage of villages destroyed by American bombs than of the atrocities committed by the Viet Cong. No one could expect the V.C. to contact an American TV crew and invite it to be on hand when village chiefs or school teachers were to be murdered. Neither was there much reporting of the nonmilitary activities of American soldiers—the material and personal assistance they gave to thousands of South Vietnamese farmers, teachers, villagers, and children—because they didn't make dramatic pictures.

Arthur Sylvester, who was for many years assistant secretary of defense for public affairs and thus the spokesman for the Defense Department, was concerned about the fact that the television news camera could "see" only a part of the action. Writing for a publication of the Overseas Press Club, he said that since the cameraman couldn't film everything, he naturally went after the most dramatic pictures. "If the men around him are being shot up," Sylvester said, "that is what he records. Yet while he is covering this particular action, it may well be that the column behind the lead company, the units on the flanks, are moving in unopposed. The casualties have been only up front—the column is quite intact. And while he shows Vietnamese civilians huddled in fear, trying to avoid the shooting, the civic action that will be taking place in this village shortly afterward probably will not be recorded because he continues to move 'where the action is.'" Sylvester's point is that while the cameraman did an excellent job, often risking his neck, he still showed only a small action out of the context of the whole. The TV viewers had only the impression of the shot-up soldiers or the huddled villagers. Sylvester said, "this immediate response to a partial story causes no end of problems." We thought we were seeing the war on TV, but the fact is we saw only selected portions of the war.

Still another fact of journalistic life that contributes to our misuse of the truth is competition, the desire for recognition and the rewards that go with it. This, too, was a part of the Vietnam coverage. Especially with the TV networks, there appeared to be an effort by correspondents to use the Vietnam assignment to establish a reputation. If one could appear to be in the midst of combat while the cameras were rolling, the folks back home would recognize him as a fearless hero of journalism, the network brass would tab him for future promotion, and the foundations would select him for honors. Thus a Vietnam assignment became an opportunity to distinguish oneself. Every correspondent, then, felt he must outdo, not only his competitors but his predecessors. Consequently, we saw a lot of crawling out of tunnels, reporting prone on the ground as bullets were heard to whiz overhead, and foreground narration of background battle. There is little doubt some of this was staged; the guns went off conveniently on cue. A large group of White House correspondents was watching one of the top news shows on a TV set in the press room one evening and broke into laughter as a former colleague dodged and ducked with the sound of gunfire as he reported on the war "as it happened." If this sort of "hoaked-up" reporting didn't contribute to a credibility gap in relation to what was really happening in Vietnam, I would be greatly surprised.

I'm sorry that our motives are not always pure. Truth is not always our only thought. We want to be successful, we want recognition, we want to make money. Not only do individual reporters want to get ahead, but papers, magazines, wire services, radio and TV stations and networks must have circulation and ratings. We must sell our product. The selection of news stories and the choice of headlines are made not only to tell a story but to sell papers and attract sponsors.

As for the individual reporter, here's an example of what can happen. Some newsmen in broadcasting work on a fee system. That is, an amount is paid for each report that is actually used on a newscast. The more stories used, the more money the correspondent makes. Consequently, the broadcast journalist, in order to "sell" his story to his editor, is sorely tempted to search for the most dramatic angle. If the editor is hard to sell, the story may become more dramatic than the facts justify. Unfortunately, this principle is not peculiar to the broadcaster. Take, for example, the free-lance magazine writer. Many a regular reporter on a beat for a paper or a syndicate exists on a very mediocre salary. It is natural that an ambitious reporter try to augment that salary, and that can be done by selling stories to magazines. The magazines are not interested in run-of-the-mill stories. They want hard-hitting, attention-getting features that aren't being printed in the daily papers. So what does the would-be magazine writer do? He seeks the sensational slant. He has a better chance of selling an article that charges the president with being an egoistic, self-serving, politically motivated, cruel, sleazy character than a less sensational, objective appraisal of the president that takes into account some other facets of his complicated personality.

A friend of mine who was a wire service correspondent in Hong Kong for years told me of a lesson he learned from a free-lancer who journeyed through Hong Kong. The free-lancer's advice was that, in order to gain attention, a writer must make strong, positive assertions of fact whether they can be adequately supported or not. At that time, the only information getting out of Communist China was second- or third-hand. The China watchers in Hong Kong had to draw conclusions from Communist news reports, from travelers coming out of China, and from rumors, which were abundant. To give the world an accurate accounting of what was going on inside China, a reporter had to admit that his conclusion was only a guesstimate based on questionable sources. But that wouldn't sell any features in the high-paying magazines, so the free-lancer's stories were laced with bold declarations that "Mao is dying," or "there's civil war in China," and the like. Mao Tse-tung, if one checks the stories through the years, died several times. That is not good journalism, but it's good business. "Authoritative reporting," it's called, but it's irresponsible. It leads to a kind of journalistic contest to be the first with the worst.

And that brings up the sin of "scooping." Walter Lippmann said in an interview, "I think that very often the troubles of the press come from a commercialized desire to get scoops, to be the first to print the news. The desire of newspapers to be the first to print particular information is corrupting to the whole journalistic process."

It may sound silly to an outsider that one news organization beat another with a story by what seems an insignificant amount of time, but scooping a competitor is extremely important to some reporters and their organizations. At their winter convention in 1973, for example, the Associated Press Managing Editors Association was told how AP had beat United Press International by a full minute with the bulletin that Vice-President Agnew had resigned. That meant that in newsrooms all over America, bells rang and lights flashed, bringing editors and newscasters into the wire room to see the AP bulletin and then to see UPI run the same story a minute later. Everybody knew AP beat UPI. One radio station may have beat another on the air with the bulletin by a minute.

Most of the radio networks have a system to alert their stations and go on the air with a bulletin report. Thus, after a hot story breaks at the White House, there is a scramble by the wire service correspondents and the network correspondents to beat one another. Radio correspondents go on the air out of breath and with scribbled notes as they try to present a fast and reasonably accurate report. The idea is not only to beat one another, but to serve the radio stations before the story begins coming over their teletype machines from AP, UPI, or Reuters.

I'll admit I like this kind of reporting. It's exciting and satisfying, but it can be abused. I've come to believe very strongly that it's much more important to be accurate and responsible than to be first. One of the best examples of the abuse of the news scoop was Jack Anderson's story on Senator Thomas Eagleton. Several reporters in Washington had heard from a person they considered a reliable source that Eagleton had been arrested on drunken driving charges in Missouri. He was the vice-presidential candidate on the 1972 Democratic ticket with Senator George McGovern and was already in trouble because of the fact that he had received psychiatric treatment. All of the reporters were handling the story in a professional way—checking out police records, conducting interviews, but reporting nothing until they had evidence. It was a question of who would be the first to break the story and get the credit for it. The shortcut way was to go without the evidence, and that's what Anderson did. He got his scoop, but he later had to apologize to Senator Eagleton, although after great damage had been done.

Related to the scoop is the deadline. Sometimes a reporter feels he cannot wait for adequate information but must file his story, ready or not.

Then there's the sin of vindictiveness if a news source doesn't cooperate to provide the kind of information we want or enable us to meet our deadlines. Richard H. Stewart, who had worked in the newspaper business for 21 years, took time off to serve as Senator Edmund Muskie's press secretary in 1971 and 1972 and ran into several situations in which he was not proud of his former profession. His first unpleasant experience, he said, was in Milwaukee. A television talk show host called the hotel at night and wanted Muskie on the show that night. Stewart told him the senator's schedule prevented it but they would try to accommodate him on another occasion. Vengeance was swift. The TV host shot back, "Watch my show tonight . . . I'll fix you . . . " Then there was a New York correspondent for a French-language paper in Canada who wanted an interview with Senator Muskie. When the request was declined, the correspondent shouted on the telephone: "Then I'll hurt him in everything I write about him until I get the interview!"

Another problem is limited knowledge. A couple of White House staff people have told me how amazed they are that news reporters jump to big conclusions from little knowledge. We see such a tiny portion of what is really happening, yet we must be experts. We must never admit that we don't know. James Russell Lowell wrote: "In a world of daily —nay, almost hourly, journalism, every clever man, every man who thinks himself clever or whom anybody else thinks clever, is called upon to deliver his judgment point-blank and at the word of command on every conceivable subject of human thought." It's not just the journalistic pundits who do this but all experts, as John Adams wrote of the Congress: "every man in it is a great man, an orator, a critic, a statesman; and therefore every man, upon every question, must show his oratory, his criticism and his political abilities."

This is one of the sins of "instant analysis," I think. When our broadcast experts are called upon to analyze a presidential speech, it would be terrible, in front of the whole world, to say "I don't know." Walter Lippmann, in his 70th birthday talk before the National Press Club in 1959, put his finger on the matter when he asked: "Is it not absurd that anyone should think he knows enough to write so much about so many things? You write about foreign policy. Do you see the cables which pour into the State Department every day from all parts of the world? Do you attend the staff meetings of the Secretary of State and his advisers? Are you a member of the National Security Council? And what about those other countries you write about? Why don't you admit you are an outsider and are therefore by definition an ignoramus?"

Former Washington columnist, Peter Edson, commenting on the same subject, warned that the reporter should not think he knows all the answers and try to run the country or dictate to it. He said some columnists give the impression of knowing all there is to know about every subject they write on. "All too often," he said, "the personal opinion columns with their big 'I think' or 'I believe' are the results of mere head-scratching, thumb-sucking, and fingernail-biting."

Another sin of the press is what I call the "wire service syndrome." In the fall of 1965, *Newsweek* magazine printed a critique of the press with the title on the cover: "What's wrong with newspapers?" It charged, among other things, that newspapers often abdicate their editorial prerogatives in favor of syndicated columnists and delegate too much of their news responsibility to the Associated Press and United Press International. In my opinion, the newsmen who select the news for the wire services and write the stories for the wire services are among the most powerful people in this country. Most radio and television broadcasters depend heavily on the news that comes into their newsrooms over their teletype machines. Where does it come from? From the wire services: UPI, AP, and Reuters. Most of the approximately seventeen hundred newspapers get their news from the same sources.

Even the major TV newscasters and reporters seem to regard the wires as the news "Bible." How many times I've been frustrated that I could not get my editors to place proper value on my stories because the wire services weren't seeing them the way I did. I would get the reply: "But the wires aren't carrying it." Or "It isn't on the wire." And the unspoken conclusion was: "If it isn't on the wire, it isn't news." Similarly, if an incorrect story is on the wire, it's next to impossible for a correspondent to get his newsroom to disregard it. A White House news story will illustrate the point: In late March 1966 there was considerable talk of inflation and ways to head it off. President Johnson was said to be considering a tax increase to take some purchasing power out of the economy and to discourage business expansion. That, it was argued, would cool off the economy and avoid runaway prices and wages. On this particular afternoon, the first lady had planned a reception in the state dining room for a group of White House Fellows, young men and women who were to spend a year as interns in the federal government. Mrs. Johnson was ill, however, so the president substituted for her in the reception line and acted as host.

After the formalities of getting acquainted were out of the way, the President suggested he would be glad to answer any questions the young people might want to ask. It turned into a regular press conference, with a few members of the regular White House press corps scribbling down the president's remarks. A question was asked about whether the president planned a tax increase. He explained reasons he would rather not, listed three ways his economic experts had said could be used to combat inflation, tossed in some figures and percentages in case a tax boost became necessary, but said he wanted to do more checking on alternatives before deciding.

When I got back to the Mutual Broadcasting booth in the west wing of the White House, my news desk was calling me for a story that had just run on the Associated Press wire about a new tax increase the president was going to inaugurate. I could hardly believe the bulletin that was read to me. AP was saying the president planned a $5 billion tax boost after the first of April. I said that was misleading and I would give them a story that I thought was an accurate interpretation of what the president said.

On Capitol Hill at that very moment, the House was debating a money bill—appropriations that had been requested by the president. A long argument was being waged over two items especially: a rent subsidy program and a teachers corps—two pet programs of the president. Republicans were demanding that the budget be trimmed sharply at this time of rising military costs for the war in Vietnam. Also at issue was whether domestic spending would add fuel to what the Republicans insisted was "spiraling inflation." In the state dining room, the president had talked privately to three of us about his irritation with these congressmen who were on an "economy jag," giving the appearance of cutting costs but actually talking about small amounts, like $10 million and $20 million, a drop in the bucket in relation to his $103 billion budget.

The irony was that the AP bulletin rolled during the height of the bitter House debate on the money bill. The House Republican leader, Gerald Ford, saw it, ripped it off the teletype and hurried into the House chamber, waving it and remarking, "Some strange things are going on in the nation's capital today." The *New York Times* the next morning reported that within minutes Democrats and Republicans had gathered around the news tickers in the Speaker's lobby to read the misleading story that the president was considering an imminent tax increase. The Republicans had added fuel to their argument that expenditures ought to be cut, rather than taxes raised.

The White House press office made desperate efforts the rest of the afternoon to correct the story, and the next morning the president made an unscheduled appearance at a news briefing to tell reporters in person: "There is absolutely no decision to raise taxes." But many media, including radio and TV, continued to use the original AP story. The stock market fell 10 points. I think the wire services perform a remarkable service and have an excellent record for accuracy, but they are not perfect.

Closely related to the wire service syndrome is the matter of news selection. Spiro Agnew thought it was bad that the TV networks have a great amount of control over what news stories are selected for broadcast. Others have charged that there's an Eastern liberal conspiracy to slant the news. But I believe it is the wire services that are more influential in selecting the news. I also reject the idea of a conspiracy. I have seen no evidence of it. However, there is something else, which might be called journalistic incest: one reporter talking to another, one reporter picking up another reporter's story, reporters sharing information and ideas.

During the U. S. involvement in Santo Domingo, for example, reporters working for competing papers roomed together, took one another's telephone calls, rode in the same cars, and exchanged information. It happens in Washington, too.

While there are differing views of what is news and what is the most significant part of a speech or press conference, there is usually a striking similarity in the treatment given the news stories and in the selection of news that goes into newscasts, newspapers, and news magazines.

Some of the sins of the press crop up as the result of fatigue or inconvenience. We used to joke about standing in the hot sun in the White House rose garden, waiting for President Johnson to come out to speak to a visiting group. We would imagine LBJ asking press secretary Christian: "Are any reporters about to faint, George?" "Not yet, Mr. President." "Then I'll wait a little while."

But if that had been true, it would have been bad judgment because unfortunately, reporters have a tendency to write unfavorable stories when they are inconvenienced. They get snappy and irritable, just like anyone else, and tend to take it out on the person who caused the inconvenience. Much of the inconvenience for White House reporters comes from travel and its uncertainty. The classic examples came up during the Johnson administration. His press secretary, Bill Moyers, told a story that illustrates Johnson's unpredictable trips. He said the president called him on the telephone one day and said, "Bill, I'm thinking of flying to Honolulu for a meeting with the South Vietnamese leaders. What do you think?"

"Well, that sounds like a good idea. I'll come and talk with you about it. Where are you?"

There was a slight pause and the president answered: "I'm over Los Angeles now."

That didn't really happen, but some other unbelievable things did. One weekend it was rumored that the president would fly to his ranch in Texas, stopping on the way at Houston to participate in the dedication of the new sports stadium, the Astrodome. Judge Roy Hofheinz was president of the organization owning the Astrodome. He was an old Johnson friend and a political supporter. What happened that day is a classic example of LBJ's handling of the press and the predicament his press secretary often faced.

George Reedy was press secretary then. He said he was pretty sure the president would make the trip, but LBJ hadn't told him definitely. Reedy knew the decision could come only minutes before departure so he had to decide whether to order a plane for the press. Usually the charter planes were sent from New York, and, presuming one of the airlines had an available plane and a quickly available crew, it would take a minimum of two hours to have it at Andrews Air Force Base near Washington. Another consideration was that it takes reporters at least a half hour to get to Andrews from the White House. Reedy knew that to order a press plane, which would cost around $10,000 for the Boeing 707, might incur the wrath of LBJ. On the other hand, if the president decided to go and the press plane were not ready, the presidential condemnation would be certain. So Reedy decided to play it safe by gambling on the cost and ordered the charter jet. To be doubly safe, he planned to have a pool of four correspondents waiting in the west lobby, totally unaware of the agonizing decision making which was going on in the press office. A secretary from Reedy's office was sent out to the lobby to notify four reporters to come into his office. I was one of them. Reedy explained that if he decided to get us to Air Force One at Andrews, we would be given a high sign to come into his office and proceed directly to the south lawn where a helicopter would be. We had been back in the lobby for a half hour or so when the sign was given and we followed the prescribed procedure. We had been told not to let our colleagues know what was happening because Reedy didn't want any premature stories. As our chopper was lifting off from the south lawn, toward the Washington Monument, on the way to Andrews, Reedy confided that he still didn't know for certain that we were going anywhere, but that he had a press plane standing by and he wanted us aboard Air Force One "just in case." Some time later, the president's helicopter appeared. He got aboard Air Force One and we took off, still in the dark as to destination. Meanwhile, the rest of the correspondents, 40 or 50 of them, were waiting at the White House. It was not until Air Force One had been in the air for more than an hour that they were told the president had left and were advised to get on a bus for Andrews. After we had been in the air for two hours, we had been told only that we were going to Texas; we still hadn't been given the word that we would stop in Houston. As it turned out we did land at Houston.

The president, followed by the press car in the motorcade, stopped at the home of Mrs. Ovita Culp Hobby for a reception, then proceeded to the Astrodome for an exhibition baseball game on the occasion of the official opening of the spectacular stadium. And that brought still another frustration for Reedy. The president and the four press "poolers" were already in the luxurious "skybox" of Hofheinz and the exhibition game was well under way before the press plane with its load of correspondents arrived at the Houston airport. Naturally, all of the reporters were anxious to go to the Astrodome where the President was, where the story they came to cover was. But Reedy's reading of the president's intentions was that he would stay for only an inning or two, and Reedy therefore could visualize the press buses coming into the Astrodome just as the president was heading back to the airport. Consequently, Reedy ordered the press to wait at the airport. It was hot, especially on the plane. Drinks were being served. Impatience turned to anger as the president stayed for inning after inning. Malcolm Kilduff, assistant press secretary, who stayed with the reporters on the plane had the assignment of trying to relay Reedy's instructions and trying to pacify the furious correspondents, who were becoming madder by the minute. Correspondents can be very articulate in their verbal denunciations of anyone, but after a time the denunciations graduated from verbal to physical. One member of the journalistic fraternity threw a right and a left at Kilduff.

Back at the Astrodome, finally, in the ninth inning, after the fabulous electric animated scoreboard had demonstrated for the president how it comes alive with pawing bulls and bucking horses—accompanied by sirens and other sound effects when there's a home run—he called it a night and headed for his limousine, the four correspondents dashing for elevators to beat him downstairs and to the motorcade cars. It was our duty to give a report of the events to our steaming colleagues, but by the time we got to press headquarters in Austin, it was well past midnight, far too late for morning paper deadlines and evening newscasts. As might be imagined the coloration of reports from Texas that weekend was almost exotic. I don't believe news stories should be colored by our personal feelings, no matter what the circumstances, but sometimes it's almost impossible to avoid.

This was one factor Richard Nixon realized when he moved into the White House. When Lyndon Johnson visited the White House one day, Nixon gave him a tour of the new press facilities, and Johnson remarked: "The press facilities have been greatly improved. Have the news stories improved, too?" I think they had, to some extent, partly because of the consideration the Nixon people gave to our personal concerns. There was a sincere effort for quite a while to give us at least three days' notice before a trip. Eventually that eroded: Nixon became upset with the press, and we were back in the rut of unpredictable travel.

Another press sin is a spirit of unreasonableness that is sometimes prompted by inflated self-importance and sometimes by naiveté. During the energy crisis in 1973 when the Nixon administration was trying to get voluntary cooperation on fuel conservation, a reporter spoke up in a briefing by press secretary Ronald Ziegler. The reporter noted that the energy shortage could boost the wool industry because people would wear more sweaters. "But," said the reporter, "out in Wyoming, coyotes are killing the sheep. What does the president think about that?" What did he expect Ziegler to say?

Try to imagine a reporter asking, "Mr. President, why did you appoint Thurgood Marshall to the Supreme Court?" Would a reporter really expect the president to say, "Well, to be perfectly honest, I did it because the polls show I'm in trouble with the black voters." We often do not expect honest answers because our questions are unreasonable.

I have asked questions of public officials that I knew beforehand could not be answered honestly, but the tactic is part of the game we play for the sake of the public record. I participated in an interview with Bill Moyers and had the first question, which was supposed to be a blockbuster or a "zinger" to get the interview off to a fast start. I put the question as bluntly as I could: "Mr. Moyers, is it possible for Lyndon Johnson's press secretary to be honest?" The question was really unfair. I would have been a fool if I had expected him to say, "Yes, Forrest, it's impossible. I have to lie, twist the truth, and deceive because the President makes me do it in order to cover up his mistakes and make him a more popular and powerful man." What I was really doing was testing Moyer's ability to give a credible answer to an incredible question. He handled it well:

MOYERS: I'm not sure that I understand that question, Mr. Boyd, because it sounds to me as if it is implying that the President would want me to be dishonest, and that's not true.

BOYD: Let me explain why I asked it. I've heard it said around the White House press room that a problem you have is that you try to be honest, and it's impossible in your position.

MOYERS: Oh now, I don't think that there is built into this job a streak of deception and the necessity for dishonesty. The appearance of dishonesty, or at least of contradiction, is very real, on some occasions when it is impossible to give all of the information that a reporter would like to have. But I do not know of one instance in the period of my service in the White House or in my period of service as press secretary when the need to be dishonest was there.

This catalogue of sins is not complete. We of the press have other faults. We are too sensitive to criticism. We have no way of censuring members who get out of line. The list could go on. In 1969, a survey for the Associated Press Managing Editors Association showed that the principal concerns of the people about the press were: editorial prejudice, inadequate research, inaccurate headlines, and too much attention to sensational news.

I can only say I am sorry for these shortcomings. I do not take them lightly, and I think we ought to try our best to correct them.

PRESIDENTS, PREACHERS, AND THE PRESS

One would think that presidents go to church to hear the truth, and that preachers try to elucidate truth. But there is a problem for both, especially when the press is in church, too.

That's why I was not exactly surprised when Richard Nixon began his administration by announcing he would have Sunday religious services in the White House. In modern times, presidents from Roosevelt to Nixon have had to exercise great care in choosing the places and manner of worship. When Franklin D. Roosevelt took Winston Churchill to church in Alexandria, Virginia, the minister embarrassed Roosevelt and angered Churchill with a lecture on colonialism. A Baptist convention condemned Harry S. Truman for gambling and drinking. Dwight D. Eisenhower almost quit going to church the day he was baptized because of the publicity given the private ceremony. John F. Kennedy had to lay down rules for a Middlesburg, Virginia, priest because the sermons had political implications. Lyndon B. Johnson once rendezvoused with a hidden helicopter on a Texas ranch to escape an after-church chase by the press. And Richard M. Nixon inaugurated services in the White House because he could not, as president, attend a regular church service without becoming a source of distraction to the congregation and the cause of all manner of special preparations, including security.

Why such a problem? In some instances, the attendance of a president has caused unmanageable crowds. In others, the public fuss has ruined the spirit of worship. Sometimes the press has made itself obnoxious by trampling flowers on church lawns, interviewing the president and parishioners, analyzing every word of the sermon for story possibilities, and writing uncomplimentary reports about the president's church manners. On many occasions ministers have taken advantage of the president's presence to gain publicity. (One veteran White House correspondent once said, "All preachers are publicity hounds.")

But there are problems for the ministers, too. The Reverend Edward L. R. Elson, then pastor of the National Presbyterian Church in the nation's capital, was besieged by favor seekers when President Eisenhower attended his church. One of the roughest times of his entire ministry, he said was just after Eisenhower took office and was asked to commute the death sentences of Julius and Ethel Rosenberg. It seemed that the worldwide Communist community tried every conceivable way to exercise influence, Dr. Elson said, and one method was to try to approach the president through his minister. The pressure was unbelievable. For a variety of causes, Dr. Elson was always receiving petitions, telegrams, and personal appeals before and after church services.

Ministers have the problem, too, of carefully choosing words and subjects, lest the reporters who follow the president everywhere misunderstand or misinterpret. The Reverend Albert F. Pereira, the young priest in charge of the Catholic church President Kennedy attended when weekending in Virginia, put it this way: "The only ones who make me self-conscious are the reporters. I now strive in preparing my sermons to avoid saying anything that—and I don't want to be unkind to the press—might be twisted or misconstrued, because of the president's presence in the congregation." Despite the fact that Father Pereira was conscious of the problem, he sometimes slipped. Shortly after JFK became president, Father Pereira started to refer to golf to illustrate a point, and President Kennedy laughed aloud because the papers had been full of criticism of former President Eisenhower's devotion to the game.

President Eisenhower ran into a peck of trouble over church attendance. He had never joined a church before he became president because, as he explained, he had never been in one place long enough. He had lived in 22 different residences before becoming president. His tenure in the White House marked the first time he and Mamie had had anything like a permanent home. Before the inauguration he and Mrs. Eisenhower began membership classes at the National Presbyterian Church, and on the morning of inauguration day they attended a preinaugural service at the church with members of their families and of the official administration family. It was something of a first. After the service, Ike returned to his suite in the Statler Hilton Hotel where he wrote out a prayer on a sheet of yellow paper. He read the prayer at the inaugural ceremony, another first.

A couple of weeks later, on February 1, 1953, the Eisenhowers were to join the church officially. One requirement of the Presbyterian Church for membership is baptism. Eisenhower had never been baptized because when he was a boy his family belonged to the River Brethren Church which does not practice infant baptism and because he was on the move by the time he became old enough for baptism. Before the public service in which he and Mamie were to be among 50 new members of the church, they appeared before the elders and made confession of faith. Ike knelt and was baptized. It was the first time in American history that a president was baptized and confirmed while in office. It was supposed to have been a private service, but because it was so unusual there was great interest. Eisenhower's press secretary, James Hagerty, said later that Dr. Elson had suggested a press release but that the suggestion had been turned down "but good!" However, it seems more news of the private service got out than Eisenhower would have liked. Some reporters had the impression that he was so irritated he was tempted to quit going to the National Presbyterian Church almost before he started. Some kind of news release had been given to the press. Dr. Elson said a written statement about the baptism service had been picked up in the church office by the wire services. He said the purpose of the printed sheet was to make sure Presbyterian language was used in the news stories describing the service.

Dr. Elson said the White House never gave him any rules to follow as the president's pastor, but he himself promised two things in a letter to the president: (1) that he would try to be a good pastor and be available to render spiritual service and (2) that he would not use or permit anyone else to use the pastoral relationship with the president for any but religious purposes. In this connection, Dr. Elson determined he would not disclose anything discussed with the president in private.

Eisenhower was severely criticized for his new church affiliation. Senator Matthew Neely of West Virginia charged that President Eisenhower's church attendance was politically motivated. Neely's public charge was a shocker. Observing that Ike never belonged to a church until he was elected president, Neely declared that the president was getting his picture taken nearly every Sunday. Everytime he looked at Monday morning's paper, Neely said, he saw the president's picture, along with a story telling that "he has been to church on Sunday." Neely declared that one great religious paper was talking more about Eisenhower than about almighty God. "When you see this," Neely said, "you will decide that he must have been an apostle, a crusader for the Babe in Bethlehem ever since he was old enough to speak or walk or talk. But you know that he didn't join a church until after he became president of the United States, and then he joined the church which I joined more than 50 years ago." Neely's charges were made in a speech before a CIO convention in Cleveland. Recalling that the Man of Galilee denounced the publican who prayed in public so that he could be seen by men, Senator Neely suggested that if the president wanted to pray, he should "shut the door" and "pray in secret," and God would reward him openly. Naturally, Neely's outburst stirred up a flurry of protests, with Republicans and ministers coming to President Eisenhower's defense. His press secretary, Hagerty, appeared before reporters and said, "I would like to call your attention to an old adage: 'What Peter says about Paul tells more about Peter than it does about Paul.'"

The big temptation for ministers is to assume that the president's presence in the congregation represents an unusual opportunity. Not only is the chief executive there, but so is the White House press. What a forum! What a chance to be quoted by the wire services, the papers, the magazines, and the networks! The classic example of this occurred on President Lyndon Johnson's visit to historic Bruton Parish Church in Williamsburg, Virginia. The president had just completed a two-day across-the-country tour of military bases in observance of Veterans Day. He wound up the tour late Saturday night in Williamsburg. He was tired and in need of rejuvenation. The next morning, he and Mrs. Johnson, with daughter Lynda and her fiance, Marine Captain Charles Robb, sat in the pew reportedly occupied by George Washington. What the president didn't know, although he had dispatched Secret Service agents to check, was that the rector, the Reverend Cotesworth Pinckney Lewis, had written a supplement to his sermon upon getting the news the first family would be in his church. Dr. Lewis told reporters later that he believed he would never have a better opportunity to raise the questions that troubled him and that "one isn't privileged to tell the president of the United States what he thinks very often." The sermon supplement was highly critical of the administration's Vietnam policy. Dr. Lewis spoke directly to President Johnson, saying the American people were "mystified" by the complex and baffling Vietnam war. "We perhaps are involved in a good cause," but "something is wrong in Vietnam." Dr. Lewis told the president that the public was confused by inaccurate, or perhaps even false, accounts of the war and declared that what was needed was "some logical, straightforward explanation" of why and how the United States was so deeply involved in the conflict. The *New York Times* observed that LBJ's tour that weekend had included seven speeches designed to provide precisely that sort of reassurance. As President and Mrs. Johnson left the church, the president gave the rector a brief smile and murmured, "Thank you," while Lady Bird told the priest, "The choir was wonderful." In this case, Dr. Lewis may have miscalculated the usefulness of the press for the reaction was almost unanimously against his ethics. Reporters repeated, with some satisfaction, the quote of an official of Colonial Williamsburg, who said Dr. Lewis' statements were in "exquisite bad taste." And that afternoon, while waiting for the president to end a game of golf and return to Washington, reporters made a game of writing humorous leads concerning the episode. First one reporter posted his lead on the bulletin board, and as the others gathered around to laugh, they were all seized with the fever to contribute. One after another, the humorous lines appeared on the bulletin board:

"The Episcopal bishop here today announced an elevation for the Rev. Dr. Cotesworth Pinckney Lewis. He has been assigned as chaplain to the Marines at Con Thien."

"White House press secretary George Christian has announced that President Johnson did not attend church in

Williamsburg Sunday. No services were held in Williamsburg."

"President Johnson announced late Sunday he has commissioned artist Peter Hurd to paint a portrait of Rev. C. P. Lewis."

"The White House has announced the prophet Isaiah will make a state visit next month to discuss matters of mutual interest. He will not stay in Williamsburg as announced."

"President Johnson said tonight: 'Extremism in defense of God is no virtue.' "

"Williamsburg (via satellite) . . . A spokesman for God said, 'Cotesworth who?' "

"Senator J. William Fulbright has announced he will make an immediate pilgrimage to Williamsburg."

"The President announced his intention to stay here through next Sunday in order to hear the new pastor at Bruton Parish Church."

"President Johnson left Williamsburg late Sunday by helicopter. As he left he was heard singing, 'Give me that Old Time Religion.' "

A long time after the Williamsburg experience, President Johnson confided to a few reporters that he respected the right of a minister to say whatever he wants but that presidents have a right not to go and listen. Needless to say, he never returned to Williamsburg, although it had been thought he was intending to make Williamsburg one of his weekend retreats.

Another Episcopal church which George Washington also attended was the scene of another ministerial "message" for another president and his guest. It was January 1, 1942. The Second World War was in full swing, and Winston Churchill, Britain's prime minister, was in Washington for consultations. Roosevelt decided to proclaim a national day of prayer and to observe the occasion by taking Churchill to a little red brick church that Washington helped found in 1773 in Alexandria, Virginia. For security reasons, vestrymen of Christ Church were sent out early that New Year's Day as "ecclesiastical Paul Reveres" to the homes of trusted members, telling them to come to church at the designated time. All they could tell the members was "be there—we think you'll find it interesting." When they had been seated, in came the president of the United States and the prime minister of Britain, to be seated in pew fifty-nine, the pew used by Washington when he attended. As they prayed for the success of the armed forces, soldiers with fixed bayonets and steel helmets paraded past the windows. Some thought the Reverend Edward Randolph Welles took advantage of the situation and lectured the president and the prime minister on the sins of their countries. He said that "none of the nations now at war has a blameless record" and described America's greatest sin as "international irresponsibility." He spoke of Britain's "past imperfections" and denounced British colonialism. These were probably the last things the two war-burdened leaders wanted to hear from a minister, and Churchill was said to have been quite angry. Roosevelt was so embarrassed he never returned to that church.

Presidents don't seem to mind, however, when ministers publicly support them. The Reverend George R. Davis, minister of the National City Christian Church in Washington, often defended President Johnson from his pulpit. On January 23, 1966, Mr. Davis assailed critics of the Vietnam war after assuring the president he had planned to make the remarks whether Johnson was in the congregation or not. Mr. Davis said he was "amazed" to hear some people calling it "the president's war." "It is not the president's war," he said. "He didn't start it, he inherited it."

Well-meaning ministers sometimes embarrassed LBJ by overdoing their support. When he showed up for morning service at the Central Christian Church in Austin, Texas, one Sunday, the minister preached on the need for social action and helping the poor. He had taken up a theme the president often expounded, but his welfare ideas went beyond those of the president. He even used the phrase that Soviet Communists abandoned long ago: "from each according to his ability and to each according to his need." After the service, a White House spokesman remarked that we had just heard "the gospel according to St. Marx."

The press was the major problem for Father Pereira, JFK's weekend pastor in Middleburg. He was preaching a series of sermons on capital sins. Right there, of course, it was natural for the White House press to pick up its collective ears and interpret the sins as those of the nation's capital. There was special attention to see if the sins of a president might come in for particular notice. Sure enough, President Kennedy showed up on the Sunday that Father Pereira chose to preach on "Avarice," making references to people who have great wealth but die without having used their wealth to benefit their fellow men. The minister wasn't aware of it, but that very week, *Saturday Evening Post* had carried an article on the Kennedys and their wealth, including the fact that they did not give large amounts to charity, choosing instead to put their philanthropic money into Kennedy foundations. The press presumed the priest had prepared his remarks as a comment on the magazine story. Father Pereira recalls that Pierre Salinger, Kennedy's press secretary, called and reminded him of the rules laid down when the president had decided to attend the Middleburg church. One rule was that Father Pereira was to read every news story available to him that had anything to do with President Kennedy. If he had, of course, he would have been more careful with his sermon on avarice. Father Pereira said Salinger called him a number of times after the president began attending his church. He said Salinger's rules were not compulsory, being more like guidelines to avoid trouble for all concerned.

Probably the series of events that got Father Pereira in the most hot water occurred in 1961 when the civil rights movement was beginning to get national attention. As he recalls it, a group of black demonstrators—a movement known as the "freedom riders"—had decided to use President Kennedy's churchgoing habits to advantage. Leaders of the movement knew that the Kennedys would be at Glen Ora on the weekend after Easter and that on Sunday the president would attend the Catholic church in Middleburg. Not only that, with him would be the press, with the TV cameras and the still photographers. If the blacks could stage a demonstration in the vicinity of the church when the president was arriving or leaving, they would gain the attention not only of the president but of the whole world. This, they reasoned, would launch their movement. They needed a bona fide issue, so they selected a small drugstore lunchroom, marched in and demanded service. They were refused, and they had their issue. Their plan was to test the other restaurants in the small town so that by the time President Kennedy came to church, they would really have something to protest. They were so certain of success that they arranged for busloads of fellow demonstrators to arrive early Sunday morning. Father Pereira's concern was that the president should not be embarrassed and Middleburg should not get a bad reputation across the nation. So he met with the protesters, then with the mayor, then with the town council, and then with the proprietors of the eating places. To the surprise and anger of the activists, he won capitulation from the proprietors, who agreed to serve everyone. Father Pereira remembers his telephone ringing all through that Saturday night. The language on the other end of the line was anything but complimentary because the whole scheme was ruined and the demonstration plans had to be canceled. The next morning, Father Pereira asked a Protestant minister friend to announce on his 9:30 radio program that the crisis in Middleburg had been averted. The wire services picked it up and the news flashed across the country. President Kennedy called the minister and kiddingly asked, "Is all well?" The priest answered that it was and told the President to come on to mass. When he arrived, he asked the priest what he would have done if the protest demonstration had come off as planned. Father Pereira answered that he would have called the president and advised him not to come to church. The priest was criticized by some civil rights people for thinking first of protecting the president and second of the civil rights cause. That, at least, is the Reverend Albert F. Pereira's version of what really transpired that weekend in Middleburg, and it illustrates another of the problems created by a president's going to church.

The Kennedys faced additional difficulties in church attendance: they had small children. They took both children to church for the first time on October 27, 1963, in Middleburg. There was not much in the newspapers the next day about the sermon, but there was plenty about the way the Kennedy children behaved. One publication reported that Mrs. Kennedy brought along a number of picture books, including *Bambi,* and that all the books were looked at during the service. John, Jr., "crawled on his knees, climbed into his mother's lap, talked out loud once, stood up in the pew once or twice, turned around to look at his neighbors, and talked to his mother. Caroline now and then spoke to her father." Any family has its hands full when it takes a two-year-old boy and a five-year-old girl to church, but when the family is the first family and several rows of reporters are watching every move with pencils poised, the problem is magnified.

The press greatly complicated President Johnson's church attendance, especially when he was in Texas. While LBJ was at the ranch, press headquarters were established at either the Driskill Hotel in Austin or the El Tropicano Hotel in San Antonio. Usually church plans were posted in the briefing room Saturday night, often as late as eleven or twelve o'clock. On Sunday morning, reporters in 30 to 35 rented cars drove the 50 or 75 miles to Johnson City or Blanco or Stonewall or Fredericksburg for the service, after which the press caravan tagged along wherever the president went. As often as not, the journey included a visit across Johnson-owned rangeland in a big cloud of dust, with the final destination being one of the ranch houses or the LBJ ranch. Then followed long, off-the-record sessions with the chief executive that were most profitable for correspondents trying to get insights into the man and his policies. Because these after-church affairs were so productive from a news standpoint, no one dared miss church, and when LBJ left the church there was always a mad race as reporters jockeyed their cars into position as close to the president's car as possible. There often was scraping of fenders and banging of bumpers. Once as the president left his boyhood home in Johnson City on one of those Sundays and entered Highway 290 for the ranch, a following car driven by a well-known television newsman was almost hit broadside by a large truck. The newsmen packed their cars together three and four abreast behind the president's white Lincoln on the Johnson City and Fredericksburg streets, running stoplights if necessary so as not to lose sight of the leader. On one chase across the Texas hill country, several cars ran out of gas. One Easter after the president attended services at the Episcopal church in Blanco, his vehicle led the long motorcade back to Johnson City and then north. A Secret Service car was sandwiched in between the presidential car and the press caravan and kept slowing the reporters as the president accelerated. Suddenly the reporters topped a hill and discovered that the president's car had disappeared. They drove wildly on, thinking they were in hot pursuit. Apparently following a well-worked-out plan coordinated by walkie-talkies and two-way radio, the president had turned onto a ranch owned by his business friend, A. W. Moursund. There a hidden helicopter waited and the president boarded it for a flight to the home of a friend for lunch, without the press. Aides drove the white Lincoln back to the LBJ ranch, without the president. It was like a chapter in an Ian Fleming novel.

Eventually the president decided to discourage the press from following him to church. Press secretary George Christian said church plans would no longer be announced, and he guaranteed that the president would not invite churchgoing reporters to the ranch after services, nor would he make any statements before or after church. A television reporter tested that one Sunday morning. Finding LBJ in the little Catholic church at Stonewall, he approached the president after the service, microphone in hand, camera crew close behind, but the president ignored him and walked directly to his car.

Reporters are still trying to figure out why LBJ quit attending the church where he had been a member since he was a teen-ager: the Christian Church in Johnson City. The last time he appeared there as president was November 20, 1966. On that Sunday, Pastor C. Ray Akin, the lay minister, announced that the 70-member congregation had voted to make Johnson an elder. Perhaps that had something to do with his decision not to attend anymore, although he accepted the election. Or maybe it was because of some misunderstanding over an air-conditioning unit he and Lady Bird had given the church. Or perhaps it was because a reporter wrote that in one service there he clipped his fingernails. He later said he had merely clipped a hangnail. Or maybe he felt that the part-time minister, the tiny choir, the teen-aged boy pianist, and the plain folks of the congregation were being ridiculed by reporters. Or as one of Johnson's aides surmised, maybe he just preferred the Catholic and Lutheran churches closer to his ranch, for he began attending their services rather regularly on Sunday mornings. Whatever the reason, the church he had attended most regularly suddenly became off limits.

President Harry S. Truman is probably best remembered for his salty language. After he used "SOB" at a Washington dinner, the Reverend Carl McIntire, then president of the International Council of Christian Churches, demanded that Truman apologize to the nation for such language.

But language wasn't the problem when the Baptist General Convention of Texas met in Fort Worth in November 1945. A resolution offered by a Corpus Christi minister and adopted without opposition by the forty-five hundred delegates stated that "because of the reported attitude of the President of the United States as a Baptist toward gambling and drinking and because of the invitation of Baylor University to confer upon him the high recognition of an honorary degree, I move that we instruct the trustees of all our colleges and universities not to confer any honorary degree on those holding to such a position." The Reverend W. L. Shuttleworth of Houston, chairman of the convention's Civic Righteousness Committee, said on the convention floor that "no Baptist school should confer a degree on a man who likes his poker and drinks his bourbon."

Despite these criticisms, reporters who covered the White House in the Truman years remember that he seldom missed church on Sunday. And one Catholic correspondent said that when traveling on Sunday mornings, President Truman always had the train stopped so the Catholics could attend mass. Truman said that when he went to church, the preacher treated him as a church member and not the head of a circus. That's the way he wanted it. In a letter to the Reverend Edward Hughes Pruden, who served as pastor of the First Baptist Church in Washington when Mr. Truman was president, Truman said: "I don't want you ever to feel that you are handicapped on your freedom of speech and expression just because I happen to be there. I want to be treated like every other citizen and every other good Baptist. One of the things I am one hundred per cent for is freedom of expression, as long as it is within the bounds of reason and decency."

The one preacher associated most with the last several presidents is the Reverend Billy Graham. President Nixon has made no secret of the fact that Dr. Graham is one of his closest friends. During the presidential campaign of 1968, some churchmen felt Dr. Graham was being used politically when candidate Nixon showed up at a Graham crusade in Pittsburgh, but Dr. Graham didn't seem to feel that way and in fact added fuel to the fire by publicly praising Nixon as a man of great integrity. And after Dr. Graham told a questioning Dallas reporter that he had voted for Nixon by absentee ballot, big ads appeared in Texas papers claiming Dr. Graham supported Richard Nixon over Hubert Humphrey. Dr. Graham was prominent at inaugural activities for Nixon, conducted the first Sunday church service in the White House for Nixon, and was named a trustee of the Nixon foundation.

Dr. Graham also was a friend of President Kennedy, President Eisenhower, and President Johnson. Because JFK was the first Catholic president, his religious activities were under constant surveillance by Protestants who were afraid he would favor Catholic causes and by Catholics who thought he would go too far to avoid such criticism. After Kennedy had been president about a year, the Catholic weekly *America* commented that he was not making excessively friendly overtures to anyone connected with his church. Catholic prelates and Catholic clergymen paid few, if any, calls at the

White House. Kennedy rarely found himself in positions in which he might have to be photographed with cardinals or other church dignitaries. Such photographs would cost the president 10,000 votes in the Bible Belt in 1964. On the other hand, "photos of the president with Protestant spokesmen like Billy Graham were pure 14-karat gold, to be laid away at 5 percent interest till the day of reckoning in 1964." The Catholics felt he was "walking too softly on too many fragile Protestant eggs."

President Johnson liked to tell the story of a Baptist who called the White House to complain about the president's association with Jews and Catholics. The caller was told that the president could not talk to him at the moment because he was swimming with Dr. Graham. The Baptist started to remonstrate further but as the light dawned he exclaimed, "You mean *our* Billy?"

Dr. Graham and President Johnson were on such friendly terms that it was not unusual for them to call each other. After one of Dr. Graham's daughters made a public statement endorsing Barry Goldwater for president in 1964, the evangelist called the president to explain that he had nothing to do with it. Then the president explained that he had nothing to do with *his* daughter's conversion to the Catholic faith and added, "It's a good thing I'm the politician and you're the preacher."

During one Graham crusade in the Astrodome in Houston, President Johnson was at his Texas ranch. The press was informed in a Driskill Hotel briefing that Sunday that the president would fly from the ranch to Houston to attend the afternoon rally. This brought a chorus of groans from reporters. There was debate over whether this was the first time a president had attended a "revival" meeting, and the reporters insisted on using the term "revival meeting" rather than "evangelistic crusade," feeling that the former phrase carried a more derogatory connotation. One correspondent for a large newspaper asked of his colleagues, "Why does the president feel he has to dignify that Billy Graham by attending his meeting?"

President Johnson had another preacher influence: Bill Moyers, a top aide and later press secretary. While Moyers had actually prepared to teach Christian ethics, he was an ordained minister and had preached some. On a few occasions he conducted devotions in the executive mansion or at the LBJ ranch when the family decided not to attend church. And Moyers was sometimes called on by the president to say grace before White House meals. It was reported and quite generally accepted that one time Moyers returned thanks in such a low voice that the president asked him to pray louder. The answer was, "I wasn't talking to you, Mr. President." A sequel to the story came later when the president invited a few reporters to join him for lunch at the ranch. The president called on Moyers to pray and said, "And this time, I don't care who you're talking to, I want to hear you."

President Nixon's innovative idea of having religious services in the White House seemed like a way to solve the churchgoing problem. But it presented some problems, too. First, there was the matter of deciding which ministers to invite and which citizens to invite to make up the special congregation. Because of the limited space in the East Room where the services were held, only about 200 persons could be accommodated. There were charges that Nixon used the services for political purposes. Other critics argued that the president really didn't want to hear the truth, that he wanted to hear nice, innocuous things that couldn't be in any way construed as pointing out any of the evils of his personal life or of his administration. One day in a regular White House briefing, a journalist in clerical garb asked deputy press secretary Gerald Warren whether any of the preachers

President Nixon had heard had offered any criticism of the administration. Warren said he wouldn't take that question, but it is true that the ministers invited to speak at the White House were under some constraint because of where they were and how they got there.

Even when a president attends a regular church service outside the White House, the preacher sometimes has a conflict over whether he should "soften" the truth. If there was anyone President Nixon could consider his pastor, it was the Reverend John A. Huffman, Jr., the young minister of the Presbyterian church at Key Biscayne, Florida. That was the church the first family attended more than any other. And because Mr. Huffman was intelligent, personable, and alert, he made friends with a number of White House aides. His influence inside the White House was much greater than most people realized. All went fine for the most part, the preacher-president-press relationship reaching its peak when the Vietnam peace agreement was reached in January 1973. One week after Nixon's second inaugural ceremony, he was again at Key Biscayne and agreed to a peace prayer service at the Presbyterian church as part of the national day of prayer he had proclaimed. The networks got wind of it and arranged to broadcast the one-hour service. Cameras were set up and it was beamed by satellite around the world.

Mr. Huffman resisted pressures to make the service an occasion for national repentance, which the so-called doves thought was in order. It would have amounted to an appeal for forgiveness for having done wrong in Vietnam. Had Mr. Huffman injected that tone, he would most certainly have embarrassed the president. He did feel a need, however, to express a sense of sorrow at the great loss of life. His prayer was carefully written and contained a number of subtleties.

The peace prayer service was generally considered a notable success, both for the president and for the pastor. But it ultimately spelled trouble for Mr. Huffman because it brought him to the attention of the national press that accompanies the president. Several White House correspondents requested and were given interviews. Then came the disillusionment. It was Easter Sunday. The papers were full of Watergate stories. Mr. Huffman had prepared a sermon titled "Are You Almost a Christian?" He wasn't certain the president and his family would attend the service, but he no doubt assumed there was a good possibility. The president did attend, and because the press hadn't seen much of the beleaguered president, many reporters also showed up. Mr. Huffman's scripture was Acts 26:28-29. It is part of the story of the apostle Paul, a prisoner in chains, making his defense before King Agrippa. Also present is Festus, procurator of Rome and governor of Palestine. Paul's defense consisted mainly of declaring his faith in a resurrected Christ, citing the fact that there were witnesses who had seen and talked with Jesus after the resurrection and reminding Agrippa that he must have known about it because "this was not done in a corner." Agrippa said, "Almost thou persuadest me to be a Christian." Mr. Huffman said this was most likely not a sincere statement, that Agrippa was actually sneering.

It was a natural thing for the press to identify a president with a king and to misinterpret "this was not done in a corner" as a reference to Watergate operations. So the story came out: "Nixon Hears An Easter Admonition." That was the *Washington Post* headline. The general tone of the news stories was that Mr. Huffman had warned Nixon he should quit pretending to be a Christian, repent of his Watergate sins, and be a real Christian. Mr. Huffman was besieged by reporters after the service, and he told them he did not have the president in mind during the sermon. Mr. Huffman has a

long-standing policy not to preach to individuals in his congregation, and that was what he tried to explain. Most reporters quoted the following portion of the sermon and kept
the president in mind: "This is Easter 1973 tough talk.
Sorry, I'd like to give a nice, pleasant talk about the tulips
coming up in the spring—the cycle of life. I don't like to talk
about sin. But let's face it. It's a fact of society and a fact of
your and my life. We can sweep it under the rug and dismiss
it, and walk out of here into the sunshine, to the tennis court,
to the yacht club, to the beach, and say, 'Well, it was nice to
be in church on Easter.' Or you can walk out of here trans-
formed individuals by the power of Jesus Christ. It is time
perhaps, for you to 'fish or cut bait.' "

It was tough talk, but the question comes: should the
preacher have toned it down because the president was in the
audience? That would have been as bad as adding something
because he knew the president was coming.

Not all reporters were content to write the Easter sermon
story. Some wanted to know more about this young preacher
who they had concluded dared to speak directly to the
president.

A *Wall Street Journal* reporter interviewed Mr. Huffman,
got copies of other sermons, and reported that the minister
usually delivered bland sermons about the virtues of positive
living but on this Easter Sunday preached a surprisingly
tough sermon on the wages of sin and the need for repentance. He concluded that Mr. Huffman's sermon was relevant
to Watergate. Going into Mr. Huffman's personality, and
possibly his motivations, the reporter noted that the minister
was "handsome and not particularly modest . . . also very
media-oriented."

With all of this publicity, Mr. Huffman's telephone began
to ring almost constantly, and the mail began to pour in—
much of it abusive, condemning him for standing up to the

president—stemming, so far as Mr. Huffman was concerned from the misinterpretation of the press. Needless to say, he developed a very cautious attitude toward reporters and for a long time refused to grant any more interviews.

A few months later, some papers carried a story saying Mr. Huffman was being transferred, leaving the implication that his church was moving him so that he would no longer be there when the president visited. However, the truth was that Mr. Huffman had been considering a change for some time. He had met with committees of at least three large churches and finally accepted a call from the First Presbyterian Church, Pittsburgh. One of the considerations for his decision was whether he had a useful role to play as a sometime preacher to the president. He concluded that the Easter sermon and the press treatment had handicapped him. On all future visits by the president, the press would be sitting "in the seat of the scornful," reading something into every word.

Mr. Huffman told me in an interview after all the excitement had settled down that right after the service, members of the White House press came to him and the conversation as he recalled it, went like this:

PRESS: Did you say this?
HUFFMAN: Yes.
PRESS: Did you say this in your sermon?
HUFFMAN: Yes.
PRESS: Well, was this aimed at the president?
HUFFMAN: No.
PRESS: Was it a Watergate sermon?
HUFFMAN: No, it was not a Watergate sermon.
PRESS: Well, then, apparently you are saying that nothing in your sermon had any relation to the president.
HUFFMAN: Absolutely not. I wouldn't say that at all, be-

cause if I singled out anyone in the congregation and say a sermon had nothing to do with them, that person might as well not come to church.

PRESS: Well, then, you're saying that you *were* preaching to the president.

HUFFMAN: No, I did not say I was preaching to the president as far as singling anyone out.

PRESS: Well, what are you saying?

HUFFMAN: I'm saying simply this: that I preach the gospel of Jesus Christ. I try to preach it as clearly as possible, as faithfully to the Scripture as possible, and I start with myself, and am a sinner. I need to repent and everyone of us in the room is under the same conditions and whatever the president wants to make of what was said this morning is between him and the Lord.

I asked Mr. Huffman if, in the light of his experience, he would advise a president to go to church for public service. This was his answer: "Since this whole Watergate matter broke, and since I see the way anything that I would say would be misconstrued, anything that would have any cutting edge, any mention of sin, any mention of repentance, any message that would call a person to a discipline of life could be implied to be a subtle or blatant attack on the president. And if he were to call me up and say, 'What do you think, John, should I be attending church during the next few months?' I would say, 'Yes, you should, but frankly, as a personal friend, you are going to leave yourself wide open to misconstrued statements, even by those men in the pulpit who love you the most and would do their best to be fair to you.' It would be impossible for any man to give a sermon without it being taken and twisted, maybe in a very well-meaning way, by the press, because I am certainly not anti-press, but it would be very difficult for anyone to say anything that had a cutting edge that could not somehow be wrapped into the huge umbrella of so-called Watergate."

Later in the interview, Mr. Huffman stated his opinion this way: "I think the answer, really, is for a president to establish a pattern of public church attendance, in which he is willing to expose himself to some of the potential, inevitable misunderstandings and live through it and ride it out. And to encourage whoever, whatever church he goes to—the minister to preach the Word of God faithfully, no matter what happens. But all I'm saying is this puts him in a vulnerable position, and I don't know that I'd want to be in that position myself if I were president. I don't know the answer, except to establish a pattern of regular church attendance in which the chips fall where they may. Other than that, I still come back to the fact, if I were advising the president at this point, I would warn him of the impossibility of anything being said that could not be misconstrued."

THE ABILITY TO LEAD

As Richard Nixon was reeling from discouraging opinion polls and editorial demands for his resignation because of Watergate, AFL-CIO president George Meany announced: "This torn and tattered administration has lost the moral authority to lead." Until Watergate, I don't think many of us gave much thought to the "moral authority" to lead. Without endorsing Meany's characterization of Nixon, I believe he raised a thought worth pondering. If a leader consistently lies, for example, followers will not believe him when he insists that certain courses of action will lead to certain results. They will not believe if told they will be rewarded for doing certain things. And it's tough to convince people they should not break the law if the leader breaks the law.

Secretary of State Henry Kissinger was asked in a press conference during the 1973 Middle East war if perhaps the Soviet Union took advantage of President Nixon's weakness resulting from the Watergate scandal. Kissinger replied that one cannot have crises of authority in a society for a period of months without paying a price somewhere along the line.

The big factor behind the many demands for Nixon's resignation in the fall of 1973 was doubt about his ability to lead, which, many argued, was seriously weakened by lack of confidence.

As a White House correspondent, I have seen many world leaders. Not only have I covered presidents, but as those presidents traveled, I have seen other presidents, emperors, kings, queens, prime ministers, premiers, military leaders, and leaders of lesser stature.

Richard Nixon liked to introduce correspondents to other world leaders. I happened to be introduced to several. One of the most graphic occasions in my mind was President Nixon's visit to Bucharest, Romania. It was the first time an American president had visited an East European Communist country. There was a kind of triumphal motorcade into the city from the airport. As usual, there were several press buses, as close as possible behind the limousine carrying the visiting American president and the host president, Nicolae Ceausescu. There was great interest in this visit, and all of the reporters were anxious to observe the reaction of the Romanian people to the American president. The reception was fantastic. We could hardly believe this outpouring of friendliness from people who had been dominated by a Communist system for years. Hundreds of thousands lined the motorcade route, waving Romanian and American flags and shouting friendly greetings. At several points, where the crowds were heaviest, the limousine stopped, and the two presidents got out to shake hands with the people in American political campaign style. President Nixon was practically mobbed by the well-wishers. Everytime this happened, many of us scrambled off the press buses and ran up to the limousine to try to hear some of the conversation and to assess attitudes and to share in the excitement. I wanted especially to record what conversation I could so that it could be played on our newscasts. The problem for reporters was that if the presidents got back into the limousine and resumed the drive quickly, we stood the chance of missing our bus, which would mean being stranded between the airport and downtown in an unfamiliar country. It was a matter of judgment—how long to stay around the two presidents observing these history-making activities, and when to leave and run at full speed back to the press bus in order to be aboard when the motorcade resumed. It was on one occasion when I gambled and stayed by the limousine a little longer than usual that Nixon called me over to the car and introduced me to President Ceausescu.

On another occasion, I covered President Nixon's visit to China. When the president was given a tour of the Forbidden City, most of the reporters went along, and because they wanted to take in every expression, every gesture, they crowded in so closely that at times it was almost impossible for the president and his host to move. While moving through this ancient landmark, the president spotted me, had his press secretary call me over, and introduced me to Yen Chien-ying, vice chairman of the military affairs commission. He was then the top military man in China.

President Nixon introduced me to a number of world leaders, and those I didn't get to meet personally, I observed at quite close range. They included Chou En-lai, de Gaulle, Hirohito, Brezhnev, Khrushchev, Brandt, Pompidou, Franco, Macmillan, Heath, Sato, Tanaka, Thieu, Meir and Nehru. As I observed these leaders, I wondered about leadership. What did these people have that enabled them to become powerful leaders?

I've decided there are different kinds of leadership and different qualities that distinguish different leaders. Not all leaders are the "out front" people loaded with personality who are always visible and who hold the titles of leadership. A man visiting this country during the 1960's made the remark that he had talked with the student leaders of a certain university. He mentioned the student body president, the editor of the school paper, the president of the senior class, and other elected leaders. My son, who was in college at that time, said he didn't think the man had talked with the student leaders at all, that the real leaders were not necessarily so visible or so obvious. He thought outsiders paid too much attention to the school officeholders who, he felt, did not truly reflect student attitudes. I am inclined to agree with that conclusion. Many times the real leaders of an institution or an organization are the behind-the-scenes people who suggest, "C'mon, let's do this." Or they are the methodical schemers who lead without people's knowing they're being led. Or they are the opinion makers who may not be in what are generally considered leadership roles. Example setters are leaders, too, although often are not recognized as such.

I've noticed, too, that not all people in positions of power are leaders. I have often thought that in business organizations we have too many bosses and too few leaders, too many people who drive and too few who lead. It is my opinion that this is one of the evils of American business: administrators and executives don't want to go to the trouble to inspire their employees. It's much easier to sit in an office and write memos on the theme: "Do as I tell you, or else." Any mediocre individual can do that. But it takes some talent to be a real leader. The tendency is for administrators to get rid of their most talented people because these people are individualistic, have creative ideas, and cause the boss to make decisions. It's much easier to call these employees "troublemakers" and replace them with people who don't ask questions and are perfectly willing to take orders.

As I said, there are different kinds of leaders and different ways to lead. There is the charismatic leader, the individual who has that indefinable something that attracts people and causes them to follow. I don't know that anyone has been able to define this "charisma," although most of us recognize it in someone else. I was told once about a minister who just "oozed" charisma. And when I met him, surely enough, I agreed, but I couldn't define what I witnessed. When applied to leadership qualities, "charisma" refers to a combination of characteristics: great self-confidence, pleasing personality, ability to articulate, and ability to project.

John F. Kennedy seemed to have charisma, but Richard M. Nixon did not. The contrast shows that charisma is not all-important to leadership. Leadership by charisma has its limitations. Kennedy had great difficulty getting legislation through Congress. Lyndon B. Johnson, who succeeded Kennedy, got record amounts of legislation through Congress, not because of charisma, but because of other factors: timing, the mood of Congress, and political skill. There was a time in the '60's when many political experts worried excessively about the possibility that no man would have a chance of being elected president who did not have charisma; and it had to come across on television. There was a great search for candidates who were handsome, who were great public speakers, and whose magnetic personalities jumped out at you on first meeting. Some thought John Lindsay ran in the Democratic Presidential primaries in 1972 strictly on his charisma. He found out that it takes more than that to win.

One of the important ingredients of leadership, as I have observed it, is the ability to recognize when and where people are ready to be led. John Kenneth Galbraith put it this way: "It is the mark of the sound, prudent leader that he never gets too far out in front. People think him reckless and they continue to be uneasy about him even when they catch up. The gifted statesman waits until the parade is about to pass his door. Then he grabs the baton and marches out ahead." One might say that the mark of a good leader is his ability to know when an idea's time has come. My opinion is that this was one of Richard Nixon's strong points, at least during his first term as president, and even before that it accounted for his phenomenal resurrection from the political graveyard to win election as president. I believe this is one of the reasons Nixon was so hesitant to accept H. R. Haldeman's resignation during the Watergate scandal. Haldeman had been so much a factor in Nixon's ability to gauge the public mood and decide when something could be done. Haldeman was Nixon's chief of staff at the White House, but I always thought he was much more. He was the man who, on behalf of the president, kept a finger on the public pulse. Many times the president seemed to be a jump ahead of other public officials in knowing what the country was ready for, and I think this sense of timing resulted in large part from Haldeman's advance work.

In 1969, not long after Nixon moved into the White House, the Nixon people began to make remarks to the effect that the campuses were getting quieter. They sent teams of young White House aides to campuses, and they came back and reported. Nobody paid much attention. Then in 1970, to everybody's surprise, the White House announced that President Nixon would speak at Kansas State University in Manhattan. It had been a long time since a president had dared set foot on a college campus because of the anti-Vietnam demonstrations and the violence. Richard Nixon not only decided to do it but announced it well in advance. He appeared in the largest auditorium on campus. It went so well that it was unbelievable. Seasoned White House correspondents hardly believed what they were seeing. The president was given an enthusiastic reception and after his speech was surrounded and almost crushed by students wanting to see him at close range, touch him, say a word to him. I was in the middle of the throng and was almost trampled, so I can testify to the degree of enthusiasm.

That was characteristic of Nixon's sense of timing. He knew not only when to make his first college appearance but where. He knew when the people would tolerate an incursion into Cambodia, although he didn't count on the Kent State incident, which almost destroyed the calculation. He knew when he could go to Peking. He knew when he could impose wage and price controls. And, along with knowing when and where, he knew how to take advantage of a situation. I suspect that in some cases he not only assessed the public mood, but also helped shape it, perhaps by influencing public opinion polls, by selling the public on a point of view, by conditioning the public through speeches by Vice-President Agnew and others, by managing news stories, by appealing to emotions in order to get responses from certain segments of the population. Sometimes, I think, the Nixon administration created an image of public opinion and then proceeded to operate on it as a fact so that it actually became a fact. The exercise had great impact on politicians.

Let me move on to the element of politics in leadership. I have already mentioned that Lyndon Johnson used politics in his style of leadership. I believe a person can exercise leadership without the use of politics, but he does not realize his full potential as a leader if he is not a master of the art of politics. This may have been a problem with John Ehrlichman and H. R. Haldeman in the Nixon White House. It seemed to me that Ehrlichman thought he could bulldoze his way through or over people and problems, using the raw authority of the White House while Haldeman thought he could do it by image making and supersalesmanship. I'm using the word "politics" in the sense of the ability to get things done, the ability to reconcile the differences of individuals in a society and get them to work together, or at least not in opposite directions. I don't think it matters how large or small an organization or society is, there has to be an element of politics in order to get anything done. Johnson was said to have been one of the greatest Senate leaders in the history of the Congress. The reason was that he knew how to get things done. He bargained. He cajoled. He shamed. He pleased. He threatened. He collected IOU's. He argued. He persuaded. Somehow, he delivered the necessary number of votes for priority legislation. Richard Nixon seemed to disdain this element of leadership, but I'm convinced it is absolutely necessary if one is to lead effectively.

There is a dash of daring and decisiveness about a good leader, too. Former Australian Prime Minister John Gorton had a good phrase for it when he commented on his party's losing the 1972 election after having been in power for 24 years: "The government did not grasp the nettle." In other words, he was saying that his government did not dare to do what needed to be done or did not seize the opportunity that presented itself. It hesitated when it should have boldly led. And the minute a leader hesitates, the vacuum will be quickly filled by another leader who will march off with the crowd following. In the novel *The Lord of the Flies,* it is hesitant leadership that causes trouble. When the boy who was elected to lead becomes indecisive and unassertive, another boy immediately takes over the leadership role and causes chaos.

Of course, a leader can be evaluated by the decisions he makes, and it is the leader who ends up making the final decisions. It is interesting to compare the decision-making processes of different leaders. There was a distinct difference between President Johnson and President Nixon in this regard, as I observed them. LBJ liked to get his advisers together and argue all sides of a problem, then reach a consensus. To make many of the Vietnam decisions, he held a series of meetings of what was called the "Tuesday luncheon group." It consisted at one time of Secretary of State Dean Rusk, Undersecretary George Ball, Defense Secretary Robert McNamara, Assistant for National Security Affairs Walt Rostow, and possibly a couple of others, along with the president. All gave their opinions and their reasons for them. Then if the president was not satisfied, he requested that one or two or more of them gather more facts and more arguments and meet again. After rehashing the matter again and again, the president evaluated the consensus on the basis of the arguments and made the final decision.

On the other hand, Nixon, as I heard it explained by a White House aide, did not want to be influenced by personalities or personal persuasion. He wanted to make his decisions wholly on the merits of the case. Therefore all arguments were put on paper, funneled through H. R. Haldeman, and perhaps edited and digested by Haldeman, then given to the president. Nixon took the written views—pro and con—to Camp David, or to a tiny island in the Bahamas, or somewhere else, where almost alone he would decide. He did not want anyone—not even an old friend like California Governor Ronald Reagan—to call him or come in to see him and persuade him for or against a certain action. That would have injected personalities into the decision-making process instead of leaving him free to make the decision strictly on the merits. It sounds like a good theory, but in practice it had the effect of isolating the president and removing him from the human influences that might have enlightened him a good deal more on the real world than he was by the papers routed through Haldeman. In the final analysis, however, it is the responsibility of the leader to make decisions. I have reservations about the effectiveness of committees for the reason that decisions are hard to come by. Some time ago on Capitol Hill, the House Committee on Committees held hearings on proposed committee system reforms. That prompted Congressman Robert Stephens of Georgia to remark that "if Moses had had a committee, he probably couldn't have written the Ten Commandments." Moses didn't write the Ten Commandments, but the point is clear.

Another requirement for a good leader is commitment to a cause. An individual who wants to be the leader just to be a big man and satisfy his ego, is pretty transparent. Would-be followers see through him. Leadership for leadership's sake is not good enough. The best leader is one who can subordinate his ego; he sees that something needs to be done and gets people to help him do it.

A leader must be steady. During one of President Nixon's lengthy visits to the Western White House, then Secretary of State William Rogers held a reception for the White House press. Rogers was staying in a beautiful home on the edge of a sand cliff alongside the Pacific Ocean at San Clemente. As he mingled with reporters on the patio, Rogers got into a fascinating discussion of leadership and observed that the United States has been extremely fortunate never to have had a manic-depressive as president. He explained that manic-depressives make tremendous leaders when they are "up"; they exude confidence and inspire people to follow them. They are irresistibly persuasive that their mission or their project will succeed. But when they are emotionally "down" and are subject to deep depression, they can become almost madmen who do dangerous, irresponsible things. Rogers said Adolf Hitler was a good example of a manic-depressive. A good leader should be just the opposite. He should be emotionally stable. He should stay on course, through thick and thin, during good times and bad, unshakable in his determination and in his faith. At the same time, he should not be overly optimistic, just as he should not be unduly pessimistic.

Let me make some comments about leadership in a general sense. First, I think it is essential to have leadership if any organization is to succeed. The church I attend in Bethesda, Maryland, is recognized as a successful church. One of our biggest problems is to find parking space for the people who want to attend the services. Consequently people from other churches in the area often ask, "What's the secret? Why is your church attracting people when others are losing people?"

I have not been satisfied with the answers I usually hear our members give. They say something like: "We are successful because we preach the gospel. We stick to the Bible." I don't think that's an adequate explanation. Many churches "stick to the Bible," and they are virtually empty every Sunday. They have no parking problems. My analysis is that the leadership is responsible. Almost universally, people who attend our church remember our pastor, Richard C. Halverson, a leader who has combined politics and diplomacy with a lot of good common sense. Also some years ago a young man named Chuck Miller came along, wanting to put some life into the youth program, and he provided leadership that attracted hundreds of youth. Not only did those kids go to summer camps, but every Thursday morning during the school year, about 300 high schoolers showed up at the church at 6:33 for green pancakes, pink milk, and inspiration before their first class. I have concluded that for every successful organization, you will always find a leader who is responsible.

I have heard some fairly serious discussions of anarchy as something to be desired, some people concluding that the problem with most organizations is management and that no management would be better than poor management. A corollary is "Petrie's Law" promoted by Robert Townsend: "Fewer people paid more tends to produce excellence at no overall cost except to the people who get fired." Townsend says, "Most of our big corporations and public institutions are dead or dying pyramids. Like fish, they're rotting from the head down. Unlike fish, they can be revived by decapitation." After quite a bit of thought on that, I believe the trouble with organizations and institutions is not that there is management and leadership, but that there is poor management and insufficient leadership.

Perhaps just as important as leadership is permitting somebody to lead. If anyone asks me for suggestions as to how his organization can become successful, I first say, "Appoint or elect a good leader," and then, "Let him lead." If that leader doesn't work out, get another, but don't interfere with the leadership once the guidelines are established. A leader must have freedom to lead. This is why I'm concerned about Congress's taking over some of the power of the president, or curtailing presidential power. The American system is set up so that a man leads for four years, and then if we're not satisfied, we elect someone else. For this reason I doubted the wisdom of the pressure on President Nixon to resign during his crisis of confidence. We have seen an era of severe challenge to leadership, for that's what rebellion is. Much of it occurred, not because of a theory of efficiency, but because of what was thought to be freedom. Freedom from restraints of any kind. Freedom from being "bossed" by someone else. Freedom to do one's own thing, as it was put. Such freedom might have its short-run pleasures, but when the fuel runs out and the food is gone and there are no jobs and no money, we'll look again for a leader with authority.

I believe, though, that the significant aspect of the rebellion against authority in recent years was a breakdown in leadership. I mean in leadership at all levels, not just at the top. In an interview with a newspaper reporter in November 1972, Richard Nixon said, "We have passed through a very great spiritual crisis in this country during the late '60's. The war in Vietnam by many was blamed for it totally. It was only part of the problem, and in many cases, it was only an excuse rather than a reason. But we saw a breakdown in, frankly, what I would call the leadership class in this country." I agree that this is where the breakdown was. We had had student protests before, we had had campus pranks, but they hadn't amounted to much. In the last couple of decades, however, our educators, our ministers, our legislators—our traditional leadership class—abdicated their leadership role. If they knew where to lead, they drew back from the responsibility. And in too many cases, the leaders led the followers to discredit leadership. Thus, the breakdown in authority. When students shouted "down with authority," it didn't mean very much. But when our leaders joined the cry, that was significant and effective. When laymen declared their unbelief, that was accepted as more or less a matter of course, but when ministers and theologians declared "God is dead" and then remained in their preaching and teaching positions, the farce was apparent.

We will only get back on track if leaders rediscover the responsibility of leadership. Charisma, enthusiasm, an ego trip are not adequate. What we don't need is the kind of leadership exhibited by the captain of a Notre Dame football team years ago. According to the legend, in the days of Knute Rockne one should never be ahead of Notre Dame at half time because the famed coach was always able to fire up his players so much during the half time that they came back on the field determined to win. On one occasion, Rockne gave his usual effective pep talk, and the captain jumped up, so stimulated that he ran full speed through a locker room door and plunged headlong into the swimming pool, the rest of the team right behind him.

There is a final observation to be made on leadership, particularly in the light of what has happened to our national leaders in recent years: it is that if leaders who are under the scrutiny of the nation through the press are to survive, they must possess, first of all, integrity. Without integrity they will not command respect. If Watergate taught us anything, it taught us that. Today's leaders must be "Mr. Clean." They must be known for their honesty and their dedication to truth. In the wake of Watergate, an administrative aide for a congressman told me he had decided that integrity was the one quality he would look for in a man he could support for president next time. I argued the point because I wondered if integrity was more important than skill or experience. For example, when I board an airliner, I don't ask how honest the pilot is. My main concern is whether he can fly that airplane. Senator Barry Goldwater declared, "Most American's don't care about the morals of their leaders as long as they lead." After considering the two views, I must conclude that in the present climate the first requirement in a national leader must be integrity. Not integrity alone. There must be the other qualities of leadership, too. But integrity must be a basic part of the mix. I know that when a leader asks his followers to follow him, they remember whether they have been tricked or lied to in the past, and if they have, they are not easily persuaded to follow again. If a leader commands followers merely on the basis of fear or power, they will follow only until they detect a weakness or an opportunity to revolt.

There is a need for caution. We must not make the mistake of looking for a perfect leader among imperfect men. After a period of disappointment in leadership, there has developed what columnist Harry Ashmore has described as a "second-coming syndrome" in which we look for and hope for a political messiah. Former White House staff member Wallace B. Henley also warned of "messianic politics." He said the clamor over Watergate fostered the search for an antidote for the cynicism and distrust that so many felt toward American politics. He declared that even our most valued institutions are simply an extension of ourselves, warts and all, and that we might as well accept the fact that even the best political leader is going to be human and will thus have limitations. It is not likely that the messiah will ever be president of the United States.

PERFECTLY CLEAR

I could not have been in the radio and television business for thirty years without acquiring some thoughts about communicating, but I have never been so conscious of communications as I have been since I started covering the White House. The president of the United States is surrounded by communications gear. Not only is the White House loaded with equipment, but every place the president goes he has communications facilities. If communications aren't available, he doesn't go. That was one of the problems when President Nixon decided to go to China. China was woefully lacking in communications facilities, having been practically out of touch with the world for years. There were just a few long-distance telephone lines to the outside world and they were not nearly plentiful enough nor dependable and secure enough for the President let alone for the traveling press. One answer was that the president's plane, Air Force One, was well-equipped with communications facilities; as he flew through the air, no matter where he was, he could pick up a telephone on his desk and talk to anyone anywhere in the world. That would work fairly well, even while the plane was sitting at the Peking airport. But the Chinese had a kind of phobia about unmonitored radio signals going out of their country, so they agreed to permit a portable ground station to be installed at the airport. It provided regular telephone service by satellite. As soon as this system was in operation, the Chinese declared that Air Force One had to stop using its transmitters. Even when President Nixon visited the Great Wall, he was never far from a mobile radio-phone that was linked to the ground station in Peking. And when he flew to Hangchow and Shanghai on a Chinese plane, Air Force One flew close behind so it could relay radio messages back to the ground station.

Wherever Air Force One lands, a white telephone that is connected with a land line and the White House communications switchboard is brought to the foot of the ramp. Signal corps personnel immediately upon deplaning pick up that phone and keep the line open while the chief executive is at the field. At the same time, press officers and Secret Service agents carry walkie-talkies to coordinate the many activities that accompany the movement of the president. The limousine in which the president rides to his destination is equipped with two-way radio.

When the president is on an island or in a foreign country, a communications ship with elaborate electronic gear stands nearby.

The reason for all this communications equipment is that the survival of the world could depend on the ability of the president of the United States to communicate. The period of greatest tension that I have witnessed at the White House was in June 1967 during the one-week Israeli-Arab war. It was felt that a miscalculation, a misunderstanding, or a deliberate action by an irresponsible party could bring the big powers into the dispute, possibly cause nuclear weapons to be used, and turn the world into a big cinder. So, when the U. S. intelligence ship *Liberty* was hit by Israeli fighters and torpedo boats and American fighter planes began taking off suddenly from our carrier in the Mediterranean, President Johnson immediately put the hot line to Moscow in use to assure the Soviet leaders that the planes were merely going to the aid of the *Liberty*. It was the first time the hotline was ever used.

One presidential trip ran into complications that could have been serious because communications facilities were not up to par. It was the time President Johnson attended the memorial services for Australian Prime Minister Harold Holt. Johnson and Holt had established a warm personal friendship, and LBJ had already visited Australia, getting a mixed welcome of friendliness and strong antiwar protests. At one point paint was thrown on his limousine. Some protesters tried to throw themselves in front of his car. Holt received considerable criticism for entertaining the American president and for supporting his Vietnam policies, but when Holt ran for reelection, he used the theme: "All the way with LBJ." Holt disappeared while skin diving off the coast of Australia, and when officials finally concluded there was no hope of finding him, they planned a memorial service.

White House correspondents were called into the briefing room one afternoon and told: "The president is going to the services for Prime Minister Holt. We'll leave early tomorrow morning for Australia. You can get the shots you'll need here at the White House this evening." I got five shots and rolled and tossed all that night with a slight fever as a result. When you fly west, the days can be 36 hours long, and Lyndon Johnson made full use of every hour. We flew and flew, stopping briefly in Honolulu, then at Pago Pago for a midnight fire dance while the planes were refueled, and arrived in Australia in the early morning hours. LBJ was raring to get to work. He used the visit to meet separately with many world leaders who also had come to attend Holt's funeral. After the funeral, we had no idea where we would go from there. We loaded into the press planes and took off, landed in Darwin, Australia, for fuel, and took off again, still unaware of our destination. We were finally told we'd land at Korat Air Force Base in Thailand and would need gamma globulin, which would be given to us aboard the plane. We were on the ground at Korat a few hours, then made another unannounced flight, this time to Cam Ranh Bay, South

Vietnam, and then off we went on still another secret mission. After a brief stop at Karachi, Pakistan, where LBJ met aboard the plane with the president of Pakistan, we took off again, with rumors that we would land at Rome where the president would see the Pope. It was on this leg that the communications problem was a factor. Because of the quick departure from Washington, Air Force One was not available; it was getting a checkup. The president used the backup plane, which did not have communications equipment as good as that on Air Force One. Consequently, security arrangements on the ground in Rome could not be made in time for the president to drive in a motorcade from the airport to the Vatican. The alternative was to use helicopters, but that, too, required arrangements to be made by radio communications. The staff and the crew of the president's plane and the Secret Service literally put the Rome stop together "on the wing," and it was not until we were within three hours of Rome that the final decision to land there was made. There were no incidents, but those responsible for the president's safety were pretty worried.

The press is constantly aware of communications facilities. There's no point in our following the president if we can't communicate our stories. At the White House, of course, there is no problem. Everybody has a telephone, and the radio broadcasters have booths and microphones with direct broadcast lines to their studios. But when we travel, especially to a foreign country, that's something else. On the trip with LBJ, for example, the stop at Korat Air Force Base was supposed to be "off the record." For security reasons, we were told, we were not permitted to file any stories from Korat; the president didn't want the world to know he was there until he had left. I had just climbed into a bunk in one of the barracks when I heard the Armed Forces Radio station read the announcement that the president was there. I was so tired that the significance didn't register. But in a matter of minutes, there was a knock on the door and the announcement that press secretary George Christian was holding a briefing outdoors. I jumped up and looked out the window and, sure enough, Christian was standing in the little courtyard between the buildings, surrounded by several reporters in all stages of dress, some in pajamas. I joined them in time to get the word that because Armed Forces Radio had broadcast the story, we were free to file our stories. Telephones, he said, were in the headquarters building, and we could get there the best way we could find. With several other reporters, I jumped on a pickup truck, and away we went to the headquarters building. Before the truck came to a full stop we were piling off and running to grab the few telephones. There were several phones, but many of them were on the same line and we were soon shouting at one another. There were only two long-distance lines out of Korat to Bangkok and then to the United States. It was in the middle of the night in Thailand but midday back home, and the world was waiting to hear where the president was. Finally, one of the broadcasters got a line to New York, and the rest of us took turns reading our reports. The one network recorded us and fed the material in turn to the other companies.

Hardly anything is more frustrating than having something urgent to say and no way to communicate it. One Veteran's Day President Johnson visited several military installations and came to rest finally on the aircraft carrier *Enterprise,* off the California coast. Reporters were told there would be no facilities for filing reports from the carrier. That was most disappointing because it would have been "good radio" just to be broadcasting from an aircraft carrier at sea, a much better story than waiting until the next day and doing the report from San Diego. One radio newsman

solved the problem by borrowing from his Los Angeles station a small mobile telephone transceiver. He set it up on the
flight deck and got a clear signal to the San Diego mobile
phone operator. After checking around, I discovered it might
be possible to get a call through to the ship-to-shore operator from the ship's radio room, and I requested an escort to
take me to the transmitter room. That was quite a journey.
The room we were looking for was something like 3-24-E.
The first number denoted the deck level and the second
corridor, and the letter designated the room. That sounds
rather simple, but even for the crew it is sometimes a problem
to find a certain room on a big ship. Our search was further
complicated by the fact that the president was aboard and a
large area was secured. It was known as captain's country.
We went down one passageway after another, about every
ten paces taking a high step through a bulkhead. We'd almost get there when a couple of guards would stop us and
say, "Sorry, captain's country." We'd back up and try to circle
the area, but coming up another corridor, we'd hear the same
story. Finally we arrived. When my turn came the radio
operator put me in contact with San Diego, and the operator
told me to hang on a minute. While I waited and put the
finishing touches on several reports of the president's activities at sea, I heard the operator tell several other ships in the
Pacific that they would have to stand by; the only available
channel was being used by the *Enterprise*. That was me. Then
she took my call and got my New York newsroom on the
line. Do you know what the newsroom editor said? "Forrest, we're kind of busy right now, could you call back
later?" You can be sure I explained that I wasn't calling from
the corner drugstore!

When President Nixon decided to go to Midway Island to
meet with South Vietnamese President Thieu, the regular advance team went ahead to survey the situation. They found

there wasn't much to survey—a few GI's, a lot of bicycles, some gooney birds, a few airplanes, no buses, no communications facilities. The word came back to the White House, and members of the press expressed their unhappiness at the fact they would be on a small island, halfway between Hawaii and Japan, with the president of the United States and the president of South Vietnam making history but no way to communicate the news. The White House took the protest seriously and went to work on the communications problem. A few days later when we arrived with the president, we found eleven RCA telex circuits to San Francisco, three Western Union International circuits to Honolulu, ten voice circuits via the communications ship *Arlington* to Hawaiian telephones, nine voice circuits via submarine cable to Honolulu, and one cable for photo transmission. Thus, when the two presidents stood outside the base commander's home after their first meeting and announced the first reduction of American troops in Vietnam, I was able to run to a press room, pick up a telephone and give my report. Because the announcement had come very close to the on-the-hour news, I was on the air with the story within about ten minutes.

Not only presidents and the press need to communicate; it's absolutely essential that all human beings communicate with one another. Howard Rutledge, who was a prisoner in North Vietnam for seven years, said solitary confinement was the worst kind of punishment. In other wars, he said, some of our POW's who were subjected to solitary confinement lay down in a fetal position and died. In his book, *In the Presence of Mine Enemies,* Rutledge says, "The first regulation in all the prisons of North Vietnam was 'Do not communicate with your fellow Americans.' The enemy knew that if he could isolate a man—make him feel abandoned—cut off . . . forgotten . . . he could more easily destroy his resistance and break down his morale." He said that to win the war against their nerves, the POW's devised all kinds of ingenious systems to keep open their lines of communications. They learned a code consisting of taps and pauses to represent each letter in the alphabet. They communicated by tapping out a message to the man in the adjoining cell who, in turn, sent it on to the next prisoner. Rutledge said sometimes a message could sweep around the cellblock faster than a guard could walk. "Communicating," he said, "was our major weapon against the enemy." The POW's even swept with a broom in code as they cleaned the compound. They dragged their Ho Chi Minh sandals in code. They pounded messages on pails. They coughed, sniffed, spit, and cleared their throats to send messages, desperately communicating. When Rutledge, after 540 days of solitary confinement, was given a cellmate, they talked nonstop for three days and nights. Rutledge spent about five years in solitary confinement, and his story is that human beings have an urgent need to communicate. They have to communicate if for no other reason than to preserve their sanity.

One of the best ways to hurt a person is to give him the "silent treatment." When he was graduated from West Point in 1973, James J. Pelosi made national headlines by revealing that he had been a victim of silence. He had been convicted of violating the academy's honor code, but the charge had been dismissed by the West Point superintendent on the grounds that a staff officer had prejudiced the case. Unsatisfied, his classmates voted to invoke silence, and for 19 months they wouldn't speak to him. That is severe punishment.

It's very interesting that God, according to the Biblical account, considered communication vital to man, and one of His most effective means of punishment was to destroy communication. As the ancient story goes, the people decided to build a city and a tower whose top would reach into heaven.

"Let us make a name for ourselves," they said. At that time everyone on earth could speak the same language, so God confused their language "that they may not understand one another's speech." "Therefore its name was called Babel, because there the Lord confused the language of all the earth and from there the Lord scattered them abroad over the face of all the whole earth." It seems as though man has been trying ever since to get back to that pre-Babel situation of one language, although people will fight rather than give up their own language.

Marshall McLuhan's global village concept leads us to think we've almost accomplished it. It is true that with communication satellites and transistor radios we can be in instant communication with almost everyone everywhere at the same time. But we have found in recent years that even with fantastic communications facilities, we are sometimes incapable of communicating. Part of the reason is that we interpreted McLuhan's writings to mean the facilities are the message, or the equipment is the message. McLuhan's thesis was that the medium is the message. It is not the message in the sense that all you have to do is appear before a microphone or a camera. For some people that may be a personal accomplishment or satisfaction, but in itself it is not communication. My son and I are radio hams. If there are any people who consider the medium the message, I think they are amateur radio operators. These people are all wrapped up in transmitters, receivers, antennas, and all sorts of associated equipment. My son told me once about an operator in a particularly good location—an exotic location for a ham because of the demand for his QSL card—who makes as many as 2,000 contacts with other hams on a contest weekend. He averaged 50 contacts an hour. My question was: what did he talk about with all those people? What was the message? Was there any content? The answer was that that was not important. The fact that the equipment worked is what was important. Not all ham radio is that way. It really becomes exciting when one helps relay a message that a doctor is needed, or that someone in an earthquake is unharmed, or that a ship at sea is in trouble. Then the message is the message.

The fact remains that many of us have become enamored with the communications media. This is particularly true of religious broadcasters. Some of them have told me with great satisfaction about how many radio or television stations carry their programs, as though the fact of being "on" radio or TV is the end. I want to ask: "Yes, that's fine, but what did you say? Who listened? What happened?"

Despite our communications explosion, one of the great problems that developed in the '60's and became known as the generation gap was that we couldn't communicate. We couldn't understand one another. In one of his speeches President Nixon said, "Old and young shout across a chasm of misunderstanding—and the louder they shout, the broader the chasm becomes." It seemed that everybody had the idea that nobody listens to a quiet man, so we all increased the volume and created a deafening noise that got lost in the noise being made by everyone else. Nobody wanted to listen. People communicated, or tried to, with slogans, placards, bumper stickers, and graffiti on walls. We did not have just a generation gap, we had a communications gap.

That was part of the alienation the young people felt. The leader of a Young Life group put it to me very forcefully. Young Life clubs have been highly successful in many high schools because, I think, they correctly analyzed the problems and came up with the right solutions. Their first step is to establish meaningful relationships among the young people. I was told that surveys had revealed appalling statistics concerning the number of high-school-aged students who had no one—not even a parent—with whom they could communicate in a confidential, intimate way. Family life had disintegrated. Parents didn't care. A leader of the Agape Coffee House in Georgetown told me that youths left wealthy homes in Maryland's Montgomery County and slept on the streets. One young boy slept in a trash box rather than stay at home. They wanted to be associated with some group with which they could communicate and identify more than they wanted comfort. Not only had their communications with people been cut off, but they thought, as Rollo May said, "God went off on a vacation," so there was no use trying to talk to Him.

Into this situation came Richard Nixon, asking that voices be lowered and promising to make things "perfectly clear." Voices were lowered. Protest died down. Violence subsided. But I'm not sure very many things became perfectly clear. I think we have begun to bridge the communications gap, but I'm not sure we've gone very much beyond just communicating. There's not much content in the message. Anthropologists now tell us that man is distinguished from animals not because he makes tools but because he verbalizes. Animals may come close to verbalizing. Two University of Nevada psychologists taught a female chimpanzee named Washee to use sign language, with a 140-word vocabulary. And a University of Oklahoma psychologist taught chimps to use sign language to communicate among themselves. The signs refer mostly to objects and events familiar in the life of a chimp. To indicate food, for example, the animal puts its index finger and thumb together to form a circle and touches his mouth. To signify fruit, the chimp places a clenched fist against his cheek. Placing both arms across the chest with each hand gripping the opposite shoulder is the sign that he wants to give or receive a hug. And scratching the back of one hand with the index finger of the other means that some tickling is desired. That's fine for animals, but man is capable of a great deal more. Animals communicate in order to collaborate and survive. Man is capable of more profound communication, but I wonder if we even begin to realize our potential. One of the deficiencies of journalistic communication—of instant analyses—is that we deal with a constant stream of information, which is an inadequate diet for the whole man. We must have something better. We in the radio broadcasting business are fond of a statement that illustrates the value of words as compared with pictures: "Give me 1,000 words and I can have the Lord's Prayer, the Twenty-Third Psalm, the Hippocratic oath, a sonnet by Shakespeare, the Preamble to the Constitution, Lincoln's Gettysburg Address, and I'd have enough left over for just about all of the Boy Scout oath. I wouldn't trade you for any picture on earth." That's an example of what is possible.

Another dimension was illustrated in a speech by Stephen K. Bailey, vice president of the American Council on Education, before the New York State regents trustees conference. He spoke of that moment in the mathematics class when the eyes of one student wander "unfocused and luminous past the teacher and the blackboard in the sudden discovery of the symmetry, the wonder, and the principled beauty of the universe." And "the mounting excitement of a student who, in catching the cadence of a line from Yeats, suddenly feels the Irish Sea breaking inside him." Bailey defined the prime function of education as restoring man's sense of his own nobility.

If man can communicate to some extent with the animal world, and if he can communicate profound thoughts and feelings to his fellow men, can he bridge the communications gap between the finite and the infinite?

In the Kaiser Aluminum publication on telecommunications, there is this observation: "There seems to be something going on inside us that we do not understand. Some sort of cosmic, transcendental forces flow through us, as if we were a telephone line." This suggests to me that all of us reach out for a more complete communications fulfillment, which may come not through blaring loudspeakers but by a still, small voice.

REALITY, FANTASY, AND COGNITIVE DISSONANCE

Erich Fromm quotes a Chinese poet: "I dreamt last night that I was a butterfly and now I don't know whether I am a man who dreamt he was a butterfly, or perhaps a butterfly who dreams now that he is a man."

It is increasingly difficult to tell what is real and what is not. This is partly because of politics, partly because of new philosophies, and partly because of the media. It's sort of phenomenal that although we have been conditioned to believe everything, we have come to disbelieve everything. The impossible claims of political candidates, the utopian promises of commercials, and the philosophies of the absurd have served to confuse us. What is show business? What is real? What is false? What is valuable? What is not? I read somewhere that this is the age of the great put-on: some day a young televiewer will grow up to be a world political figure and someone somewhere will threaten to drop the bomb. Our boy will reply, "You're just putting me on." And someone will drop the bomb.

Some of the confusion in knowing what is real and what is fantasy is genuine. Some is deliberate. In some cases, people prefer the unreal to the real. Sometimes we honestly can't tell the difference.

Contributing to the confusion is our fascination with images. An image of something or someone can be more important than the real thing. So far as public opinion is concerned, what is perceived is what counts. We can turn around

113

the old saying "What you see is what you get" and make it
read: "What you *think* you see is what you'll vote for."

In my younger days, I thought I was opposed to the idea
of image making. My attitude was that I would be myself
and do my assigned job well, and people would recognize
that fact without my having to call their attention to it. I
would not try to impress anybody. I finally discovered that
it doesn't always work that way. In more pessimistic mo-
ments, I concluded it hardly ever works that way. The person
who gets the good job, the one who gets promoted, the one
who is recognized, the one who gets elected is the one who
makes some effort to create a favorable impression.

I believe a reluctance to sell oneself or to permit oneself to
be sold has kept many good people out of political life.
They would consider it demeaning and even hypocritical to
become engaged in the image business. John Quincy Adams,
the great, great-grandson of President John Quincy Adams,
gave a speech at the White House during the Lyndon Johnson administration. He said his grandfather ran for governor
of Massachusetts five times but never made it. He concluded
that the Adamses since President Adams were simply "unable
or refused to allow themselves to develop an ability to communicate effectively with the man in the street." He said,
"We may have been strong on principle, with all its virtues,
but I'm afraid we haven't been able to accept the fact that
Madison Avenue, like it or not, is almost as necessary a part
of the political process as a sound background in the classics
and a keen sense of history. This failure to face the world as
it is, and not as we would like to have it, has been, I feel, a
tragedy." It is an intriguing thought that Adams spoke of
facing the world as it is when he was talking about a world
that wants images.

Richard Nixon expressed somewhat the same idea. Almost
every new man who joined the White House staff said,

"We've got to humanize the president. We've got to make him appear to be more of a warm person." Then Attorney General John Mitchell, who was a political adviser to the president, said, "The president isn't getting across the way he should. People don't see him the way they should." Nixon's associates thought the image perceived by the public was that of a mechanical and calculating man, all business and no heart. There was a group in the White House that met occasionally to plan activities Nixon could engage in to improve his image. But Nixon said, "These public relations experts always come in and are constantly riding me. 'You have got to do this, that and the other thing to change your image.' I am not going to change my image. I am just going to do a good job for this country." In a television interview, President Nixon said, "When presidents begin to worry about images, when they begin to be concerned about polls, when they begin to read their press clippings, do you know what happens? They become like the athletes, the football teams and the rest, who become so concerned about what is written about them and what is said about them that they don't play the game well. The president must not be constantly preening in front of a mirror, wondering whether or not he is getting across as this kind of individual or that."

Despite his statements, many people believe Nixon was the most conscious of image of any president. Thus we had *The Selling of the President 1968,* the book written of the Nixon presidential campaign by Joe McGinniss. It quotes Hubert Humphrey as having said, "I'm fighting packaged politics. It's an abomination for a man to place himself completely in the hands of the technicians, the ghost writers, the experts, the pollsters and come out as an attractive package." But Humphrey found out that people vote for images. It may seem that I am preaching heresy, but how else can people vote? In a country as large as ours, it is impossible for candidates to personally meet enough people for a long enough period to let the people really know what they're like and what they stand for. The only way to get to enough people in the available time is through the media. Theoretically, at least, the candidate who uses the media best is the winner. When a voter sees the candidate through the media, it's almost impossible for him to judge whether he's seeing the real candidate or an image. Thus from a political standpoint, if a candidate wants to be a winner, he must first determine, through the use of opinion polls and other samplings, what the people want. Then he must project or sell the image that conforms to that desire. A candidate may get the votes of the people on the basis of the image that he projected, but if he is to have the trust of the people, that image must be backed up by reality as time passes.

Richard Nixon was conscious of image throughout his presidency. It was common for people to ask about the "real Nixon." There were stories now and then about the "new Nixon." Whenever he was in public, he was on stage. Whenever he stepped off Air Force One, he wore that perpetual smile. Whenever he stepped into a room or onto a platform he exhibited that smile, that quick step, those waving arms. He instructed members of his family to do the same. Outside a church in Newport Beach, California, after the wedding of his niece, the president whispered to the new bride to always smile because there were cameras all around. I used to wonder why those Nixon masks worn by pranksters or protesters always startled me. Then one day as Nixon walked out of the Oval Office into the rose garden with a distinguished visitor, I realized it was because he always seemed to be wearing a mask with a frozen smile.

The image committee even got to Mrs. Nixon. Not long after the Nixons moved into the White House, it was decided she needed a new image. So they hired a new press secretary, enlarged the press office staff and increased the budget in order to change Pat Nixon's image. I guess it worked. They made changes in her hair style and her clothes. They scheduled foreign travel for her and arranged meetings with the press. And presumably, Mrs. Nixon became a more valuable asset to the Nixon administration, not because she became a different person, but because she was perceived to be different.

For a while, there was a concentrated effort to show the Nixons more as a family than they had been pictured before, more as down-to-earth home folks. The result was pictures of the president with his Irish setter and of him and Mrs. Nixon strolling along the beach.

Lyndon Johnson had his image makers, too. Some insisted that he must not wear glasses when he made TV appearances. Some decided, apparently, that he should project a sweet, grandfatherly image. They insisted he must use a teleprompter, sometimes even for nontelevised speeches. They built a special podium for him that had all kinds of gadgets —the arms to hold the teleprompter mirrors, a motorized, elevator-like platform so that his height was exactly right, lights, microphones, a clock—and the podium was transported everywhere LBJ went to make speeches. He was so dependent on it that the press dubbed it "mother." The Johnson image makers were always experimenting and tinkering so that he came over many times failing to project a positive image and consequently was unconvincing as he tried to rally support for his Vietnam policies or his domestic programs.

Image can apply to ideas and issues as well as to people. A thing can be made to look like something it isn't. John Ehrlichman, onetime domestic counselor to President Nixon, once said it is important to avoid even the appearance of wrongdoing. It is even possible for the truth to be perceived

as untrue—and the other way around. In his letter of resignation, Ehrlichman wrote, "I have always felt that the appearance of honesty and integrity is every bit as important
. . . as the fact of one's honesty and integrity."

Image can also be illusion. Letters and telegrams that
come to the White House after a presidential TV address,
for example, can appear to represent a spontaneous outpouring of support and can be made to appear to represent
the majority American opinion. The fact may be, however,
that the letter and telegram campaign was organized by the
White House itself. The illusion can then inspire a genuine
response that cannot be separated from the illusion. We're
constantly drawing conclusions from situations like that.

We usually think of image making as a public relations
operation. "Puffery," we call it. An experienced journalist
can spot a "puff" piece immediately because, while it appears
to be a "straight" news story, it is 100 percent favorable to
a person or a product. It is usually written in return for
some kind of favor and should have the word "advertise-
ment" written above it. But there's another side to this coin.
Instead of failing to practice what we preach, John Kenneth
Galbraith says we sometimes "fail to preach what we practice." He was referring specifically to the U. S. policy toward
the Soviet Union in the 1960's. He said the government was
actually on rather friendly terms with the Russians while
publicly preaching a strong anti-Communist line. That was a
case in which image did not measure up to reality.

There's another way to consider reality and fantasy. There
is a common belief that seeing is believing. But that isn't
necessarily so. *Newsweek* correspondent Charles Roberts in
his book, *The Truth about the Assassination,* wrote that the
assassination of President John F. Kennedy in Dallas taught
him that eyewitness testimony is the worst kind. He said,
"Victims of horror—no matter how eminent they are—suf-

fer also from faulty recall." He concluded that the more that is written about the assassination on the basis of eyewitness recollections, the more his suspicion is confirmed. Reporters on the press buses just a few car lengths behind the presidential limousine disagreed as to what they saw and how many shots they heard.

I believe that even more true than "seeing is believing" is "believing is seeing." Abraham Vereide, founder of the International Christian Leadership movement, used to speak of "doing the impossible, seeing the invisible, and believing the incredible." One doesn't have to think in theological terms to grasp that we live by faith, "the evidence of things not seen." That is not wishful thinking or fantasizing. It is more a matter of comprehending the fact that unseen things can be more real than things we see and, therefore, more believable, although someone who doesn't "see" the invisible reality would call it unbelievable. As a matter of fact, don't we often describe the realities of greatest worth as "unbelievable"? We usually follow that exclamation with "fantastic!" It is a mistake to limit our conception of reality to only what is visible.

To take this a step further, we can be oblivious to even visible realities because we fail to see them or because we don't look. I have read with great interest the Tolkien books about the hobbits, and my mind has sometimes expanded the incident of Bilbo's entering the dragon's tunnel where gold and jewels lay all around. I have questioned how it would have been had there been no light. He could have been surrounded by incredible riches without knowing it. Perhaps with a small, narrow-beam flashlight he might have picked out a diamond or even a bracelet. But with a big light, he could see the whole room full of riches. I think we tend to go through life without a light, and I guess if I had just one prayer, it would be: "Give me vision to see what there is of value around me. Give me insight to understand what there is to understand."

When a person refuses to face reality, he is practicing what has been called "cognitive dissonance." It is fooling oneself: "let's pretend the trouble isn't there and maybe it'll go away." I understand it was Leon Festinger who proposed the theory of cognitive dissonance in 1957. It has to do with rationalizing one's behavior, doing what one wants to do and finding facts or theories to justify it. "Dissonance occurs whenever a person simultaneously holds two inconsistent cognitions," Elliot Aronson explained as he illustrated applications of the theory in *Psychology Today* (May 1973). Aronson gave this example: A smoker who is confronted with evidence that smoking causes cancer will be motivated to change either his attitudes about smoking or his behavior. The former alternative is easier, so the smoker may decide that the studies are incorrect. He may point to friends who smoke and conclude that smoking can't be all that dangerous. "He may conclude that filters trap all the cancer-producing material. Or he may argue that he would rather live a short and happy life with cigarettes than a long and miserable life without them. The more a person is committed to a course of action, the more resistant he will be to information that threatens that course."

During a vacation in South Carolina, my wife and I noticed flashing lights outside one night. It was like lightning, but without thunder. At the time there were a number of reported sightings of unidentified flying objects, or flying saucers. My wife said something about going out to see what the light might be, and I said that if it might be caused by a UFO, I didn't want to look. I never want to see a UFO so if there's any possibility I might see one, I'm not going to look. That's cognitive dissonance. It's a refusal to know the truth or arguing that what is true is not. They say man is a rational animal. He is also a rationalizing animal.

This was one of the causes of the energy crisis. It was believed that the country knew it was coming for 20 years but didn't do much about it until the crisis developed. Dr. Carl Dyrud, a University of Chicago psychiatrist, observed, "We are very sensitive to the idea of there being any outer limits." Therefore, he suggested, we shut out the very notion. Americans, he said exhibited "fantastic denial" in failing to plan for the energy crunch. John Cunniff, the Associated Press business analyst, said denial is occurring all about us. Population is expanding perhaps faster than the world's ability to feed and clothe the new people. The car-highway-pollution-congestion syndrome is destroying cities, but solutions are avoided, and masses of people continue to crowd into metropolitan areas. We don't want to do anything about these inevitable crises because we don't want to think about them. T. S. Eliot said, "Human kind cannot bear very much reality."

There are many examples of such unwillingness to accept the truth among various leaders. Sometimes it can serve a purpose. It can be a sign of bravery. But cognitive dissonance can be a form of cowardice or stupidity. Unwillingness to believe bad news is an example. One of Lyndon Johnson's most frequent criticisms of the press was that it always emphasizes the bad news. Spiro Agnew's theme during his first years as vice president was that the bearers of bad news ought to be censored. One of the comments I heard often from people I met was: "You fellows write too much bad news. Why don't you report some good news once in a while?" I spoke to a breakfast group in downtown Washington one morning, and, as usual got a number of questions on "why is it that you people report so much bad news and so little good news?" One man cornered me, got on the elevator with me, and continued the discussion on the street. "If you newsmen would just report the news right, you could change the world in a day," he argued. I agree that for various reasons the news media tend to emphasize the bad news—the crimes, the scandals, the tragedies. But at the same time, I don't believe publication of an event should be ignored just because it is bad news. I also disagree with the theory that only bad news is news, but I can't go to the other extreme and contend that only good news is news. We have to know the truth, even if it hurts.

The sin of rejecting bad news is not modern. We can go back over thousands of years, to Jehoshaphat, king of Judah. Through marriage, he allied himself with Ahab, the king of Israel, and they decided they would join in an attack on Ramoth-gilead. But before attacking, Jehoshaphat said to the king of Israel, "Inquire first for the word of the Lord." So, the king of Israel assembled the prophets, some four hundred of them, and asked, "Shall I go to battle against Ramoth-gilead or shall I forbear?" They told him what he wanted to hear: "Go up," they answered, "for the Lord will give it into the hand of the king." Jehoshaphat wasn't quite satisfied that the advisers were of one voice, so he asked King Ahab if he didn't have another prophet. Yes, said Ahab, "but I hate him, for he never prophesies good concerning me, but evil." But Jehoshaphat persisted, so they brought in Micaiah and asked him whether they should wage war on Ramoth-gilead. The two kings were seated on their thrones, clothed in their royal robes. The messenger who brought Micaiah briefed him on the good news predictions of the other prophets and advised him to agree with them. But after King Ahab urged him to tell the truth, Micaiah told the king that not only would his forces lose, but he would be killed in the battle. Ahab turned to king Jehoshaphat and said, "Did I not tell you that he would not prophesy good concerning me, but evil?" But Micaiah wasn't through. He told the king that the "good news" prophets had all lied as part of an evil plan to entice the king out to a battle he would lose. The king of Israel ordered Micaiah locked up, and given only bread and water. The two kings went into battle, despite the warning, and although Ahab was disguised, he was hit by an arrow. According to the account in the Old Testament, "And the battle grew hot that day, and the king was propped up in his chariot facing the Syrians until at evening he died."

George Reedy, who was one of President Lyndon Johnson's press secretaries, said in *The Twilight of the Presidency* that the presidency is actually a monarchy and the life of the White House is the life of a court. In that environment it is difficult for the monarch to get truthful information. In discussions, someone may play the devil's advocate, but "a dissenter always starts with half his battle lost." No one ever says "go soak your head" or "that's stupid." In other words, if I understand Reedy, no one wants to tell a president what he doesn't want to hear, just as Ahab's prophets assured him he could win the battle. Reedy said that there may be some truthful advisers, but in a battle between White House courtiers and advisers, the courtiers will win. He concluded, "This represents the greatest of all barriers to presidential access to reality." Another White House staff member, who served in both the Johnson and Nixon administrations, told me that even the president's inner circle of advisers is isolated from reality. They are picked up in the morning by White House limousines and delivered home at night by limousines. All day long they talk to one another. Their telephone calls are placed by operators who begin the conversation by saying, "This is the White House calling." He said the only thing that saved him from this isolation was the fact that he had to go home on the bus occasionally.

If anything characterized the real problem in the Watergate scandal during the Nixon administration it was that no one would tell the president the bad news. John Mitchell, the attorney general who became head of the Nixon reelection committee, testified that he purposely did not tell the president what he knew about it. One had to suspect that somehow the president or top aides on his behalf had created a "don't tell me" attitude.

Josh Billings said something like this: "It's better to know nothing, than to know what ain't so." That's probably true, but there are many people who would rather believe a lie than hear the truth. This preference for fantasy exists to such a degree that many people become confused. And it is difficult to distinguish the real from the unreal. So many people play games. So many live their images rather than themselves. And just as we seek real truth, we seek authentic people. What we are all looking for is authenticity—the real thing, real people. We're fed up with imitations. We have become disillusioned with plastics and synthetics. We have come to detest hypocrites. We want no part of phony causes. We're tired of put-ons. Diogenes went out with his lantern, looking for an honest man. I believe we're now looking for the authentic man.

Although we as individuals may have some trouble projecting a representative image, we must in the final analysis be true to ourselves and to what we know is true. "And," as Shakespeare wrote, "it must follow as the night the day, thou canst not then be false to any man." Beyond a certain point, we have to forget about image and about vindicating ourselves. President Lyndon Johnson used to carry with him a quotation from Abraham Lincoln. I have a framed copy of it, signed by LBJ: "If I were to try to read, much less answer, all the attacks made on me, this shop might as well be closed for any other business. I do the very best I know how—the very best I can, and I mean to keep doing so until the end. If the end brings me out all right, what is said against me won't amount to anything. If the end brings me out wrong, ten angels swearing I was right would make no difference."

I like another Lincoln statement: "I desire so to conduct the affairs of this administration that if at the end, when I come to lay down the reins of power, I have lost every other friend on earth, I shall at least have one friend left, and that friend shall be down inside of me."

THE HUMAN PREDICAMENT

The press misses a great amount of significant news by merely skimming the surface of current events. A fault of instant analysis is that it shoots history on the wing and fails to observe the causes of the events. If we were serious about our search for truth, we would have to be more conscious of what humanity is all about and why society is the way it is. We would be more expert in our understanding of man and human nature. We would evaluate government programs in the light of people and not of so much money and organizational structure.

Therefore, I think it may be worthwhile to discuss my observations of human nature and what it has to do with the news we report everyday.

When President Nixon visited the Soviet Union in 1972, he was to fly with Communist party chief Leonid Brezhnev from Moscow to Kiev in a Soviet plane, the equivalent of Air Force One. But there was a long delay because the pilot wasn't quite satisfied with the way the engines were performing. Finally, not being able to work out the problem, they had to switch planes, to the embarrassment of the Russian leaders. Henry Kissinger, consoling the aviation secretary, said, in effect, "Oh well, it's the theory of the evil of things." And he explained that if you drop a coin, it always rolls away from you or falls in a crack. Or if you drop a slice of bread, it always lands buttered side down. The theory is also known as "the perversity of inanimate objects." I doubt that there is any validity to the theory, but I do think there is such a theory applicable to mankind.

I once interviewed British historian Arnold Toynbee, and he said something I'll never forget: man's greatest problem is himself, and underlying all basic human problems is what he called "the cussedness of man." There's something in man that is sometimes evil. The real problem of society, I think, is exactly as Toynbee put it: "the cussedness of man." Various idealists have thought unrealistically that increasing reason, increasing technical conquests of nature, and increasing education would make for moral progress, that historical development means moral progress. But it hasn't worked out that way. There's always the human flaw: greed, selfishness, laziness, indifference, indolence, corruption, pride, lust, envy, jealousy.

Dr. Paul Tournier wrote of "the myth of progress," his contention being that mankind does not progress to perfection. He discredits the belief that from "the technical development of law it is expected that peace will come; from technological improvement will come a new art; from a more advanced science of economics will come prosperity . . . All the discoveries, all the conquests, all the institutions of humanity do not alter its true problem." Tournier concludes with a quote from Dr. Alphonse Maeder, "Behind all the convulsions in the political, economic, social, and cultural spheres there is the crisis of man himself." Retired columnist Walter Lippmann analyzed the 1972 presidential election as a rejection of the Jacobin or Rousseauistic philosophy: "By that I mean the belief that man is essentially good and can be made perfect by making the environment perfect, and that the environment can be made perfect by taking the mass of people to spend money for improving it." Lippmann's belief is that man is improvable, but not perfectable.

One weekend President Johnson invited all of the Latin American ambassadors to the LBJ ranch, and on Sunday they and the president went to the San Fernando Catholic Cathedral in San Antonio, where they heard Archbishop Robert E. Lucey preach about the morality of the Vietnam war. He quoted several popes to support his thesis. The next week, the student newspaper at St. Mary's College in San Antonio ran an editorial critical of the archbishop. One sentence was the key to much prevalent thinking: "Surely all are on the side of peace and justice, just as all are on the side of motherhood." That, in my opinion, is a wishful assumption not supported by experience. Not every one is in favor of peace and motherhood. There are rascals. There are scoundrels. There are belligerents who will take what they can from others. That's why we have police forces and armies. That's the human predicament: the cussedness of man. Legislation alone can't deal with it, nor can prosperity, nor can science, nor can education. It's another dimension. President Johnson used to say that we could eliminate the causes of crime and war if we could eliminate poverty, hunger, disease, and ignorance. I can't agree, and I don't believe LBJ would have wanted a literal interpretation of his words. Never have we had so little poverty and so much crime. Johnson himself once observed: "The taste of affluence will sour with fear. No more bitter irony that a people so committed to the quest for human dignity should have to pursue it in trembling, behind locked doors."

On that dramatic night of March 31, 1968, when he announced he would not seek another term, President Johnson said he had made the decision because of what he termed "the division in the American house" that was a peril to "the progress of the American people and the hope and prospect of peace for all peoples." He spoke of the suspicion, distrust, and selfishness among our people. A few days later, talking with some reporters informally, the president explained his decision in more detail. He said that he could see the making of catastrophe all around. He could see the

raw elements of hatred and prejudice, of division and dema-
goguery and disorder all around carrying a blind race of men
over the brink into a nuclear age.

Others stated the danger even more strongly. Desmond
Morris, the British zoologist who wrote *The Naked Ape,*
once made this statement: "We are, to put it mildly, in a
mess, and there is a strong chance that we shall have exter-
minated ourselves by the end of the century." The basis for
his pessimism was a prediction that the population of the
world will increase at a terrifying rate, causing uncontrollable
aggressiveness.

LBJ knew he could never create a law that would make
men good, but he had a dream of greatly improving life in
this country through his Great Society programs. He was so
proud of Great Society legislation that he had all of the pens
he used to sign the bills put in a glass case and displayed in
the press area of the White House. This caused Russell Baker,
the *New York Times* columnist, to write a column on "the
historic internal happiness act of 1966." Baker quipped that
the bill was signed at Disneyland and threw the full weight
of the federal government behind man's ancient battle against
depression, blues, boredom, Sunday morning letdown, lack-
luster marriage and inferiority complex. Baker said the new
legislation established a new cabinet agency, to be called the
"Federal Happiness Administration." There was a new secretary of serenity, joy and contentment, and there would be a
Happiness Corps, made up of college-trained extroverts; an
office of Happy Operations; a Gloom Intelligence Agency
known as the GIA, tapping telephones and using trick mirrors to ferret out hidden brooders, and an Internal Happiness
Service to collect a new glum tax.

Although the idea suggested by Baker's column was pre-
posterous, I thought perhaps I had found an example when
President Nixon visited China in February 1972. There they

were talking about the "new Maoist man," who does not steal, does not lie, does not take drugs, and in whose society there is no prostitution and no corruption. He is dedicated to serving his party, his country, and his fellow man.

A good illustration was published in the official government magazine, *China Reconstructs*. It's a story, titled "In the New Society: the Tale of a Shirt." This is the way it went:

"Lao Liu of the Limin Tailor Shop in Tientsin arrived early for the morning shift. As he was sweeping up after cleaning the sewing machines, he found a length of pale yellow thread on the floor. This seemed to him rather unusual, since yellow thread was rarely used in their shop. Perhaps someone on the night shift had worked on a yellow blouse, he thought. Lao Liu was a Communist party member and very conscientious. The matter still troubled him. When he finished sweeping he looked through the garments sewn the night before. Nothing with pale yellow thread. But there was half a spool of yellow thread in the drawer of one of the machines, which meant that it had been used the night before.

"Could it be that under the electric light someone had taken the yellow thread for white? Lao Liu went through the order book and found that one garment—a white shirt—had been sewn the night before and taken away immediately. The name of the customer was Chang Kuo-tung and he lived at the Tungfong Apartments. Liu took the matter to Old Chao, the director of the shop. 'We should be responsible to our customers,' Chao said. 'If this is what happened we should get the shirt back and redo it with white thread.' The other workers, who had gathered around, agreed.

"Liu got on his bicycle and was soon pedaling among the green trees and rows of red brick buildings of the Tungfong Apartments. He found the number, but before he could knock, the door was opened by a woman of about thirty, obviously in a very upset state.

" 'Does Comrade Chang Kuo-tung live here? I've come about a shirt . . . '

" 'Oh, do come in. I was worried about how to get it to him. It's so good of you to take it.'

"Lao Liu was a bit confused. Then he learned that in two days her husband, Chang Kuo-tung, a seaman, was to leave on a Chinese freighter bound for Africa. Needing a new shirt, he had gone to the Limin Shop, which is open day and night. In view of his immediate departure, the staff had given him especially fast service; in less than two hours the shirt was ready and he took it away. Chang had left for the port immediately but in his hurry had forgotten to take the shirt.

" 'Are you leaving on the same ship?' his wife asked.

" 'Er . . . no. I'm from the Limin Tailor Shop. We made this shirt for him, but we think we used the wrong thread, yellow thread. If we did, I'll take it back and resew it with white thread.'

" 'Oh, I thought Kuo-tung had asked you to come for it,' Chang's wife laughed. 'I really admire your spirit of serving the people wholeheartedly.' She opened the shirt. It was indeed sewn with yellow thread. 'I don't suppose this matters very much,' she said. 'If you don't look closely you won't even notice it. Anyway, there's not much time. He sails tomorrow.'

"Lao Liu was firm. 'We'll do everything we can to get it to him before he leaves.'

"Back at the shop Liu and Chao carefully took out all the yellow thread and resewed the shirt with white thread so neatly that it didn't even look like it had been redone. At six o'clock in the evening they finally finished. Liu wrapped up the shirt and left on the run for the railway station.

"It was three o'clock the next morning when he got off at

the port station. The buses were not running so he had an hour's walk to the seamen's lodgings near the docks. As he approached he could see the ships of many colors anchored in the harbor, and in the distance the red flag flying atop a brightly lit Chinese-made freighter being loaded by cranes, ready for departure.

"When Lao Liu found Chang Kuo-tung, the seaman was just about to leave.

" 'I've brought your shirt,' panted Liu.

" 'Why, what a surprise!' said Chang. 'How is it that you brought it? Are you shipping out today, too?'

"Liu had to explain that he was from the tailor shop, and told the whole story.

" 'You really do put Chairman Mao's teachings into practice,' said Chang, grasping the other man's hand. 'I can learn a lot from your strong sense of responsibility.'

"Lao Liu saw the seaman aboard. With a long whistle, the ship pulled out just at sunrise. It was a good start for the day."

That may sound elementary and farfetched, but it's the kind of morality we encountered during our visit to China with President Nixon. We found we could leave our hotel rooms unlocked with no fear of theft. I left recorders and cameras out on the desk. Sometimes I left the key in the door and when I returned, one of the boys at the desk, having hung it in its place, handed it to me. Some think China is the only country in the Orient where valuables can safely be left in hotel rooms.

We could hold out a handful of money when paying for something and a clerk would take only the amount required. You can't do that in Europe, or hardly anywhere else in the world. It's interesting that other Communist societies are not the same in this regard. There's a marked difference between China and the Soviet Union, for example. While visiting the Soviet Union, I was approached more than once on the street by black marketeers wanting to give me rubles for dollars at a much better exchange rate than I could get officially. And while there's hardly any visible crime or juvenile delinquency in China, there is a juvenile delinquency problem in the Soviet Union. One Soviet publication stated not long ago that every third ambulance call in Moscow is for the purpose of picking up a drunk. Drunkenness and rowdiness are major problems in Russia—but not in China.

One of the best and funniest examples of Chinese honesty was well-publicized at the time of the Nixon visit. It concerned the impossibility of throwing anything away. The most-told story was that of one of our group trying to get rid of his thermal underwear in the wastebasket as he left his room one day. The next day the underwear was back, laundered and ironed. As he packed for departure from Peking, he decided to try again to get rid of the underwear in order to save room in his suitcase. I was sitting in front of him on the bus as we were about to leave for the airport. On the bus came one of the hotel boys and down the aisle to the reporter. "You forgot your underwear."

We found evidence of this new Maoist man in various circumstances. At a transistor factory, we questioned a young man about his work, his salary, his savings account and the possibility of getting an increase in pay. He told us it is possible to get more money by putting out more work and doing it better, but he declared he does not look at it that way. His motivation for more and better work is not to get more pay, but to better serve the people, the party, and Chairman Mao.

At a hospital in Shanghai, I met two young girls, one whose arm had been cut off in an accident, the other with four fingers cut off one hand. The doctors had rejoined the severed limb and the fingers and the girls were able to go back to work. One told me, "I can say my hand was given back to me by the party . . . by Chairman Mao, and I am determined to use that hand to serve our country, to serve our society, and also to contribute to the building of socialism."

One of the doctors who had performed the operation said, "It is only under the leadership of the Communist party and Chairman Mao that this could happen . . . a severed hand could be rejoined."

This theme, "serve the people," was to be found everywhere. It bothered me, I'll confess, because it appeared that Mao and the Communist party had changed human nature, and that seemed to destroy my theory of the cussedness of man.

But as I have thought about it and learned more about what has happened in China, I have concluded there is something unreal about the new Maoist man. He's not quite what he appears to be.

First, there has been a long conditioning process that might have made B. F. Skinner proud. It starts with military-like discipline of the very young and continues through providing security for the very old. Small children march in formation to and from school, for example, with teachers and children barking out orders. In downtown Shanghai at noon, I took movies of a class of children going either home or to lunch. They marched in formation across the street when the light changed, then marked time on the sidewalk as a young "officer" stood in front of them and gave the commands. They went through several maneuvers before the little boy gave the "at ease" order and off they scattered in all directions. This early discipline teaches an obedience that we can't conceive of in this country.

Another part of the conditioning is the constant bombardment of propaganda. During a visit to an agricultural commune, I was walking across the grounds with an interpreter and a representative of the commune when the loudspeakers atop tall poles began to blare forth "The East Is Red." I asked how often this happened and was told, "Three times a day—morning, noon and evening."

"Why is it played?"

"It is to tell the people's commune about the policy of the central committee of our party, and also educate the people in Mao Tse-tung's thought, and to tell the commune members about the situation of the revolution and of promotion and production of the whole commune."

I was told "The East Is Red" is played over the government-operated radio stations three times a day, also, so that every Chinese gets the message.

When I visited the home of one of the commune families, I did not see a radio or a television set, but I saw a loudspeaker over the door. It was a bare speaker, not even in a case. I assume it was connected to some central programming source at the commune so that whatever the leaders wanted the family to hear was piped in over this speaker.

The indoctrination permeates everything, even the schools. If anyone thinks American education is serving someone's purpose of indoctrination, he ought to go to China. Most of the classes, it seems, center on Chairman Mao's thoughts.

There are also huge billboards along the streets, at the airports, and in buildings. They carry the thoughts of Mao and other slogans as constant reminders of the party line. Most of the people wear Mao buttons. They carry the little red books of Mao's sayings.

The indoctrination even continues in the entertainment. The ballets are called revolutionary ballets because they are always built around a story of the revolution or a hero of the revolution. So the revolution is also the theme of sports, literature, art—you name it, it praises Mao and socialism.

Another potent tool behind the creation of the Maoist man is the thought control. Those who are disgusted with the American press should be thankful that at least there is some diversity. It is possible in most parts of the United States to read or hear more than one point of view. When Vice-President Agnew criticized the television networks for the fact that the editing and choice of news were decided by a small unelected elite, he may have been saying something that needed saying, but the fact remains that the networks are not under the control of one central clearing agency. Many reporters, many commentators, many writers, many cameramen, many producers are involved. More than that, there are independent TV stations with their news departments and commentators; there are radio networks and independent radio stations; and there are newspapers and magazines, along with books, and the exchange of information, ideas, and opinions in other public forums. In this country, "media" really is plural. Someone pointed out to me that the term "underground press" is laughable because the so-called underground papers are sold on the streets. There is amazing freedom of the press in this country, and if one has sufficient interest, he can quite easily find and read a wide spectrum of opinion, from the far right to the far left. We've taken it too much for granted. There is no central control of all media. But in China, all news that the people get is funneled through the New China News Agency: Hsinhua. The government controls the news the Chinese people get, except for what they may hear through foreign radio broadcasts, such as the Voice of America and the BBC. Not only are the newspapers and magazines controlled, so are the radio and television programs and news broadcasts. For all practical purposes, the people of China hear and see nothing that is not approved by the government.

Coupled with this conditioning and control is a certain

benevolence, and the government is constantly reminding the people of what is being done for them. The government is paternalistic: it makes sure the people are not hungry and not too cold and that their health needs are met. They are constantly being told how much better things are now than they were "before liberation." It is a system of reinforcement. A member of the revolutionary committee for a factory in Peking told us there are three criteria for improved salaries: seniority, productivity, and political behavior. The political behavior, it seems, can cover a multitude of activities. The principle is: "Be a good Mao follower, do good, and you will receive your reward."

But even this is not enough, in my opinion, to produce the honest, sober, serve-the-people Maoist man. There is also, I think, an effective system of surveillance and punishment. It's difficult to learn much about the punishment, but I'm convinced it's there. After three reporters had interviewed the priest at a Catholic church in Peking, during which the priest said he heard several dozen confessions per week, we wondered among ourselves what the penance might be when a parishioner confessed to having done wrong. One of my colleagues quipped: "Probably three 'Hail Marys' and five years in jail." I don't know what the jail situation is. But something happens to people who get out of line. A professor at Peking University told me about the "sins" of the former Chinese Chief of State Liu Shao-chi. I asked where Liu is now and was told only, "He isn't here anymore." When I asked about Lin Piao, the deposed defense minister, I got the same answer: "He isn't here anymore."

We do know that people are sent to May 7 schools for "reeducation." There are various guesses as to how much the schools are regarded as punishment, but my feeling is that people do not look forward to being separated from their families for long periods while they spend their time in what amount to work camps.

I also suspect that punishment for wrongdoing can be swift and severe. Speaking on the occasion of the twenty-eighth anniversary of the Communist party in China, Mao said, "When anyone among the people breaks the law, he too should be punished, imprisoned, or even sentenced to death . . . " *U. S. News & World Report's* book, *A New Look at Red China,* said: "In 1952, Mao waged the '3 anti's campaign' and the '5 anti's campaign.' The first was directed against 'corruption, waste, and bureaucracy.' All government departments were to participate. Officials found guilty of any of the three sins were to be given 'penalties ranging from dismissal, prison terms, and labor camp terms to death sentences.'

"The '5 anti's campaign' was aimed at tax evasion, bribery, cheating, and theft of state assets or state economic secrets, and was used to liquidate 'bourgeois elements' in the cities, such as the merchants and people who had owned factories. As before, the decreed penalties were prison, 'reform through labor,' and execution."

Finally, the new Maoist man is isolated. Below a certain layer of officialdom, the Chinese people are unaware of what's going on in the rest of the world. The masses are kept ignorant. As nearly as we could determine, the students aren't taught comparative theories or ideologies. They get just one line. This may be calculated to cause contentment. "If you don't know there is anything else, you won't want anything. You can't covet what you don't know exists." Perhaps that helps explain how the Central Committee can control the people.

These are some of the factors that explain to me the new man in China, the ordered behavior whose tenets border on the ethics that guide Christian living. It appears to be, as another traveler to China expressed it, "a Jesus movement without Jesus."

But having built the case for the new man and having explained how he could be, I have to say that I don't believe in him. There is not really a new man. Only on the surface do the people act like new men. Chairman Mao and his Communist party have not really changed human nature. They have not made men good. They have not brought the millenium to China. Rather, they have brought a regimented society. They have succeeded in manipulating and controlling behavior. I am convinced that underneath the surface the Chinese people have the common human tendencies. But they are kept in line by the constant surveillance, the discipline, the control, and especially the fear of punishment, so that they are a nation of robots or automotons who go this way or that when the strings are pulled and have the barest minimum of freedom.

Underneath there is unrest and an ever-present potential for blood and disorder, which explain the frequent purges. And there may be more crime than we know. Henry S. Bradsher, correspondent for the *Washington Star-News,* wrote after visiting China that there is crime in China, especially among young people who have grown up under communism. He said the main problem is with youths who were removed from school during the cultural revolution and sent to farms. Some returned illegally to the cities and supported themselves by crime. Bradsher noted that farmers have watchdogs, bicycles are locked up when parked, and pickpocket operations, theft, and robbery have been reported in Canton. He recounts a report on Kunming Radio of "a directive of the Yunnan Provincial Committee of the Communist party, which held up store clerk Yen Chia-pin as a heroic example: "A class enemy tried to rob the cooperative store and Yen sought to 'protect state property.' Stabbed three times, Yen managed to wound his attacker before dying."

As China opens up to the world and becomes less isolated, I predict there will be more and more reports of trouble and crime.

It is still true, I think, that the test of a new man is his performance in circumstances that provide a choice. A man must be free to choose to do wrong before his doing right has any merit. And I think it is still true that only the power of God can create such a new man.

So I return to the fact of the human predicament, the human condition. I say that all of the attempts to fight poverty, ignorance, war, crime, and even disease are limited and in fact superficial if we do not consider the dimension of the problem that involves human nature. Isn't it strange that we are almost always dealing with secondary causes of our problems? We spend a lot of time and money adding safety features to cars but say very little about the alcoholism that is responsible for a big percentage of the accidents. We talk a lot about alcoholism as a disease but do nothing about alcohol itself. It's something like saying that a person cries all the time and that when a doctor is asked to diagnose the problem, he says the problem is that the person cries all the time.

I wonder if the Nixon administration's law-and-order emphasis didn't fall short in this regard. When he was still vice president, Spiro Agnew addressed the communion breakfast of the Holy Name Society of the Police Department of New York City and included this paragraph: "When it comes to the point of whether this Nixon Administration, and particularly myself as an individual, are going to prefer the kind of diligent, strict law enforcement that's necessary to protect this country of ours, or whether we're going to agonize over the root causes of conditions that are constantly used as an excuse for some people to commit crime, I'm going to stick with law enforcement every time."

I think General Douglas MacArthur was much closer to the truth when after a Japanese surrender ceremony at the conclusion of the Second World War, he said, "Our problem is theological." I think many people agree with that. At a conference of Marxists and Christians in Czechoslovakia, Milan Machovec said, "The question of the meaning of human life will be the essential question in the future of Marxism." He was saying, "We must understand ourselves." The root of our problems, as I see it, is human nature—the thing that causes the ills and troubles and holds us back from worthwhile pursuits; it requires an adequate, relevant treatment. I know of no better way to describe the problem than to use the theologians' label the "propensity to sin." Sin is different from lawlessness because it has to do with morality. It's more basic. Consequently, logically, I know of no better cure than to deal with sin. To be more specific, moral redemption is essential. Any columnist, any commentator, any analyst of any profession who attempts to diagnose the problems of a society without getting to this depth is missing an important element.

Albert Camus, the Algerian-born French author and moralist, groped for secular saintliness without God. So far as I'm concerned, we have learned that is impossible. Just as we told ourselves that if we were to be intellectually honest, we must discard old beliefs if we concluded they were without foundation, so now to be intellectually honest, we must be willing to accept those old values and beliefs if logic and the facts lead us back to them.

NATIONAL SECURITY, ENDS AND MEANS, AND HIGHER LAWS

There may be endless debate over whether the Senate select committee's hearings on Watergate and campaign practices were worthwhile, whether the net result was plus or minus. But the hearings were an education. A lot was said and implied about ethics—of individuals and of offices such as the presidency. Constantly cropping up were the questions of what constitutes national security, whether the ends justify the means, and whether there are sometimes higher laws to be obeyed than the laws of the land.

These topics are all related. President Nixon's claim that some laws could be circumvented in the interests of national security definitely entailed the proposition that the survival of the nation is of greater priority than laws that prohibit wiretapping. This argument also was a form of "the end justifies the means." And some of the witnesses who were involved in the Watergate operation and the cover-up said they felt at the time that they were serving a higher law than the laws the rest of us were expected to observe. Some of the senators on the committee and many commentators and columnists were quick to condemn this theory. There could be no higher law, they said. The end cannot justify the means. The witnesses were only rationalizing their unethical behavior.

An interesting exchange of views developed between the

former deputy director of the Committee to Reelect the President, Jeb Magruder, and his former ethics professor, William Sloane Coffin, Jr. While Magruder was in the witness chair before the Watergate committee, he tried to explain to the senators as to how anyone could have engaged in such a thing as the Watergate bugging. He digressed to observe that Mr. Coffin had been quoted as saying, "Well, I guess Mr. Magruder failed my course in ethics." Magruder said that was probably correct, but: "He tells me my ethics are bad. Yet he was indicted for criminal charges. He recommended on the Washington Monument grounds that students burn their draft cards and that we have mass demonstrations, shut down the city of Washington. Now here are ethical, legitimate people whom I respected. I respect Mr. Coffin tremendously . . . We had become somewhat inured to using some activities that would help us in accomplishing what we thought was a legitimate cause."

Mr. Coffin had taught ethics at Williams College. At the time of mass antiwar demonstrations and then the Watergate hearings, Mr. Coffin was chaplain of Yale. When contacted by *Time* magazine to comment on Magruder's statement, he said he would still flunk him on ethics. "Poor old Jeb never learned to tell the differences between civil disobedience and violations of the Constitution by the administration." He added: "Magruder ended up lumping all lawbreakers together. By that way of thinking, Jesus and Jimmy Hoffa are two of a kind." Mr. Coffin said that Magruder "had never examined the possibility that sometimes there is no way to test the constitutionality of a law except to disobey it. You could say that however pathetic our [antiwar] efforts were, we were trying to keep the nation under law or under God, whereas Jeb and his cohorts were trying to keep it under Nixon."

An analysis of Mr. Coffin's statements, I think, shows that

he used pretty tricky logic. He was, in fact, saying almost exactly what Richard Nixon was saying when he justified wiretaps and surreptitious breaking and entering in the name of national security. Magruder, too, was in effect justifying Watergate for the same reason Mr. Coffin cited: to keep the nation under law or under God.

Mr. Coffin's thesis is that there are different kinds of law-breakers. I'll go along with that, but the fact remains that many people who condemned Magruder and Nixon for claiming they were following a higher law were doing the same thing. They were living under the theory that the end justifies the means. This was true of the civil rights activists led by the Reverend Martin Luther King, Jr. It was true of the antiwar activists led by Mr. Coffin and others. It was true of the Protestant movement led by Martin Luther. It was true of the American Revolution led by George Washington and other founding fathers.

It is nonsense to say that there is no higher law or that the end does not justify the means. I was in a discussion group in which a man from the Pentagon declared, "The end doesn't justify the means," and it seemed to me an inconsistent view. Anybody engaged in war lives by the rule of higher law and ends justifying means; otherwise, he would be guilty of murder, trespassing, stealing, and many other transgressions of law.

What it boils down to is: "what ends justify what means?" And that, probably, is what Mr. Coffin was saying. He was saying that Magruder drew the line at the wrong place. Magruder even agreed with that, but he thought Mr. Coffin drew the line in the wrong place, too.

The fact remains that we all live by higher laws. I was almost shocked once when I read, "Necessity knows no law." This can't be right, I thought. But the more I considered it, the more I realized the statement is at least partially true.

A man rushing his dying child to a hospital will break almost every law in order to get his child there in time to save his life: red traffic lights mean nothing; speed limits mean nothing. The father is living by a higher law: necessity. If a man's child is starving, we would probably be less than ready to say the man is justified in stealing food, but he might very well think it justified.

One of the prime examples that the civil rights leaders and the antiwar protesters often cited to justify their breaking of laws was Hitler's Germany. They argued correctly that it would have been proper to disobey the laws Hitler laid down and to oppose his administration. A higher law than the law of a country sometimes prevails; in this case it was the simple law of morality.

President Nixon, therefore, by claiming national security as the reason for circumventing some laws was on solid ethical ground, I think. The Watergate committee chairman, Sam Ervin, kept condemning such reasoning by making it appear the president claimed to be "above the law." But that was not the case as I saw it. Attorney John J. Wilson challenged Ervin every time he brought the subject up: it was not a case of being "above the law" but of obeying a "higher law"; in this case, the survival of the nation.

The principle was involved in the "May Day" arrests in Washington in 1971. Tens of thousands of antiwar demonstraters had swarmed into the nation's capital, many of them determined to close down the government. During morning rush hour they were deployed in the streets, and elsewhere, to cause a massive tie-up so that government employees could not get to work. District of Columbia Police Chief Jerry Wilson, therefore, instituted a method of arrest that would take the protesters off the streets quickly. At the next press conference, I asked President Nixon if he felt keeping the government running was so important as to set aside the civil rights of the protesters. For some reason, he did not seem prepared for the question and dodged it and three follow-up questions. I had thought he could have answered by saying the end did justify the means, that the survival of the nation was involved, and that it was necessary to institute unorthodox arrest procedures because that was the only way to prevent a shutdown of the government.

My point is that there has to be some kind of higher, or ultimate, law that governs our behavior. I don't mean that everyone ought to consider civil disobedience or any other form of breaking civil laws, but I do think each person is responsible for ethical behavior based on a concept of what is morally or spiritually right. Often, this higher law is more strict than the civil law. I think it is particularly important that we recognize this in an era of permissiveness and ever-increasing freedom, at least so far as the civil law is concerned. There are many things people *can* do, and if we eliminate the restraint of what we *ought* to do, the prospect is frightening. As a society, we could be like a busload of people careening down a highway without a responsible driver. With the increasing ability of our scientists to manipulate mankind by genetic selection, the question is not whether they *can* do certain things, but whether they *ought* to. We have to live by a higher law.

I know there is danger of going too far in justifying what we do for survival. In fact, B. F. Skinner's very reason for suggesting that the behavior of mankind be controlled was survival. He contended we must trade freedom for security. We are confronted with such difficult choices that we must be very careful lest in trying to avoid one evil, we create something worse. There are many serious, intelligent people who contend that unless we are manipulated we will destroy ourselves. A great debate was begun in Michigan when a so-called incorrigible prisoner volunteered to submit to psychosurgery, a brain operation that would change his behavior and make him nonbelligerent, nonviolent, noncriminal. The surgery was held up by groups who protested that such an operation was tampering with a man's nature. Once we begin, we could end up with everybody's lining up regularly for behavioral-control shots, or taking pacification pills, or undergoing group treatments, or even having brain surgery as children. The result would be a completely controlled society as envisioned by Skinner, designed to cause everyone to live together in harmony. There would be no more war, no strife, no violence. It sounds beautiful, but I'm afraid of it, and I wonder, as others have, who will control the controllers? Thomas Henry Huxley once wrote that "if some great power would agree to make me always think what is true and do what is right," he would consent to "being turned into a sort of clock and being wound up every morning before I got out of bed." Here again, survival is more important than freedom. And for more people today, behavior control—whether in the form of electrical stimulation of the brain, monitoring devices, genetic engineering or drugs —is a threat to freedom. In the book, *Requiem for Democracy? An Inquiry in the Limits of Behavior Control,* Marvin Karlins and Lewis Andrews contend that as technology advances we may be faced with a choice: a state they call "psytocracy," in which all things, including people, are subject to careful and precise manipulation to ensure the smooth functioning of the socioeconomic system; or our participatory democracy, in which the goal is individual fulfillment.

We may indeed face a world in which the only choice left for man is between thugs and zombies. If the ultimate choice is put to us, whether anything is of higher priority than survival, I must say, "Yes, there is something." There are some things I will not surrender: my integrity, my self-respect, my freedom. They are more important than survival.

WHAT DOES IT ALL MEAN?

Many times, in all parts of the world, piling back onto the press plane after a hectic schedule of presidential traveling, speech-making, and personal appearances, White House correspondents have often asked: "What does it all mean?" Sometimes this question would come up often during the course of a particular trip, and it received a variety of answers. Sometimes it would be: "It means we're in deep trouble." Or, "It means the president is trying to sell us a bill of goods." Or, "It means the public is stupid." But I think the answer I have heard most was: "It doesn't mean anything." And some of us probably felt at times that "nothing means anything."

I think that sums up a general feeling about the last decade. We lost a sense of meaning. We did a lot of things. We took part in a lot of protests, or tried to stop a lot of protests. We supported one cause or another. We worked hard, or we played hard, but what did it all mean? Where did it get us? Education didn't make sense. Government lost its meaning. We lost our identity. The work ethic, the rat race, seemed silly. More and more, we were becoming the pawns or the slaves of technology—the machine. Nothing meant anything.

Because of the lack of meaning, there was a popular movement toward existentialism as a philosophy of life. People —especially the young—discounted history because they claimed it didn't show that man found answers that would be useful today. And our leaders were not able to show we were going anywhere worthwhile in the future. Consequently, they were left only with *now,* this moment. The existence of the nuclear bomb was always in the back of our minds as a reminder that there might not be a tomorrow. *Now* is the only time capable of having any meaning. So there was an all-out effort to maximize the enjoyment of *now.* Some of the kids thought they could do this by taking mind-expanding drugs, by free sex, by complete abandonment of responsibility, by a deliberate blindness or lack of concern about the future consequence of what they were doing at the moment, and by as total a freedom as they could attain from any kind of authority or restraint.

The NOW generation has lived long enough to produce its own history, and young people nowadays don't have to listen to someone over 30 to know that it was shortsighted and illusory. Charles Reich's idealistic book, *The Greening of America,* was out of date before it was placed on the bookshelves. The "movement" he spoke of in such glowing terms was already turning to something else, realizing its goal was a flimsy, foggy dream. Young people with stars in their eyes as they camped on the Mall in Washington for huge demonstrations, woke up in the morning to find their billfolds stolen from their sleeping bags. Others found they had to call on the hated police to protect them from violence. And then, Dr. Herbert Marcuse, who was considered the father of negative thinking and a great influence on the worldwide rebellion against authority, made one of the significant statements of the early 1970's. He said, "I completely reject the argument that universities should be destroyed because they are pillars of the establishment . . . you can still learn what you need to learn in the universities." And he added: "One doesn't cut off the branch on which one is sitting." The end of the "movement" was confirmed once and for all when John Lennon said in an interview for *Rolling Stone:* "I no longer believe in myth. The dream is over. I'm not just talking about the Beatles, I'm talking about the generation thing. It's over, and we gotta—I have to personally—get down to so-called reality." *Christian Science Monitor* writer Melvin Maddocks wrote in March 1971, "Few voices from the underground still make a virtue of Now."

But these kids of the '60's taught us some things. They made us see how ridiculous we have been in some respects. They exposed our hypocrisy, even though they may have been guilty in their own way. And if they didn't provide the answers, they at least caused us to ask a lot of questions.

Now that the "movement" is dead, there may be a sense of relief for most adults, but pronouncing the end of it does not in itself answer our search for meaning. I don't believe we will find it until we find purpose. If everything, including ourselves, is here purely by chance, purpose and meaning that stand all the tests of a searching soul are impossible to find. Man-made goals serve a limited purpose.

Not even the moon is a worthwhile goal that provides lasting meaning. Apollo 11 astronaut Edwin E. Aldrin, Jr., the second man to walk on the moon, wrote a book titled *Return to Earth*. He said that after his lunar journey he sank into a mental depression that left him paralyzed and listless. He was unable to cope with the sudden loss of a major goal or objective. I think one of the saddest things that can happen to a person is that at an early age he has accomplished all of his goals. The problem is not that he is too talented, or too fortunate, but his goals were inadequate.

President Nixon, speaking to a VFW convention in New Orleans, quoted Napoleon as saying that what is worse than losing a battle is winning one, because of the depression that follows. In a sense the purpose of existence is over for a man when he has won his battle. The challenge is gone. The battle is won. The moon has been reached. The season is over. What is left?

Absence of proper goals means boredom. I have heard it said that the ultimate crisis of culture is the crisis of boredom. George Sanders, the British actor who won an Academy Award after having scaled what might be called the "Thespian pinnacle," lived a very active life, had no money problems, married four wives, including two of the Gabor sisters, but killed himself with an overdose of sleeping pills. He left a note saying, "I am committing suicide because I am bored." What was left to challenge him?

Purpose and meaning are also related to usefulness. The members of a discussion group I attended one time were asked what they most wanted. Some suggested "to be happy," and similar generalized desires. But an analysis showed the consensus to be "to matter." To make a difference. I bought a card in California with an essay on it, titled "My Creed," by an unknown author. The last sentence read: "The purpose of life is to matter—to count, to stand for something, to have it make some difference that we lived at all." If I understood the primary frustration of the school "cop-outs" of the '60's, it was that they had an extreme sense of futility. They felt they had something to contribute, but nobody cared. Nobody listened. They were just statistics. I saw a motto in a little country gift shop in South Carolina that expressed the idea this way: "Will it matter that I was?" One great man is said to have looked back on his life and observed that he had been plowing in the water. That's something like shoveling smoke, and it really means that living hasn't made any difference to anyone.

I'll admit that it's difficult sometimes to see any useful results of one's life. One of the old-time comedians used to say, "I feel so unnecessary." Think of those people who are in occupations where they spend a lifetime with losing causes. Doctors and nurses who do most of their work with incurable patients; teachers who work with children who can't learn; psychologists whose patients have no possibility of being rehabilitated; ministers and missionaries who see no converts; wardens whose prisoners are incorrigible; coaches whose teams always lose. Aren't their lives wasted? Aren't their lives meaningless? Not necessarily, but such persons have to have a strong sense of mission if they are going to overcome strong temptation to be discouraged.

It is because of this need for meaning, and the failure of most circumstances to provide it, that I am compelled to believe there is somebody bigger than I, and something more than *now*. Otherwise the temporary friendships, the values I didn't have a chance to appreciate fully, the fulfillments *I* couldn't realize, the inequities I have seen, the injustices I have witnessed, would tell me that life doesn't make sense.

Not only have we, as a society, lost meaning, but we have lost direction. We have lost our way. Henry Kissinger, accepting the award for Very Distinguished Public Service in 1973 at the Federal City Club in Washington, said, "Nothing is more urgent than a serious, dare I say compassionate, debate as to where we are going at home and abroad." And, "only as we regain a sense of direction can we heal our nation's spirit and recover our unity." It's terribly disconcerting not to know where you are. When Lyndon Johnson was president, there were times when the press corps did not know where we were going. One day we were told we should board a press bus at the southwest gate of the White House, or meet at the MATS terminal at National Airport. Once at the airport, we were put aboard a plane with an air of mystery. We all asked each other, "Where are we going?" It was not until all of the doors were shut and the plane was taxiing that we were told. I used to think that there would come a time when we would go some place with the president and we wouldn't know where we were. There were times when it was not clear to me where I was. After some of the more exhausting trips with presidents, I have found it difficult to decompress. Especially after foreign trips that have involved long days, time differences, with many places to be and many stories to cover, then a long trip home. After an around-the-world trip with LBJ, we were back in Washington for about half a day and then he decided he wanted to do his resting at the LBJ ranch, so off we went to Texas. Richard Nixon did essentially the same thing. He had been back to Washington only one day from his trip to China in 1972, and off he went to Key Biscayne, Florida. The morning after we arrived in Florida, some of us were talking in the press room in Miami about the difficulty of knowing where we were. We would wake up in the middle of the night with a start, and practically panic, because we couldn't remember where we were or whether we should be running for a bus. Someone suggested we ought to make a big sign and hang it over the bed, so that we could flip on the light and read: "You are in Miami. Everything is all right. You don't have to be anywhere."

We should be asking ourselves, as individuals, as a nation, as a society, "Where are we, and where are we going?" If we are to find the answer to the question, "What does it all mean?" we'll have to look for some guidelines. We're at a kind of crossroads, I would say. We're at a place of collecting our thoughts and trying to put some pieces together. We're trying to get our bearings and to regain our sense of direction. Dr. Kissinger once had a good explanation, I thought, for the reason we had lost our sense of direction. He had had some frequent and unpublicized meetings with educators and students during the protest days. He remarked in a briefing that he was quite torn up sometimes by his conversations with his former colleagues. He felt that what we were seeing among the students was quite largely the product of the education system. "We've de-bunked the system for years,"

Kissinger said. "We took the clock apart, and now we don't know how to put it back together." To put it another way, I think he was saying that professors, and other leaders, removed the traditional landmarks and put nothing in their place. We're still trying to figure it out. We're asking some serious questions. To paraphrase the cigarette ad about women having "come a long way," we are wondering if we really have come a long way. How much have we really progressed since the caveman or Stone Age man? We seem to be at that uncertain place—the carnival ride swings to the top of an arc and we could go on around or fall backward, and about all we know is that it's impossible to stay in one place. We hardly know which way we want to go, or what we want. We just know that where we've just been is not "where it's at."

We are at the point of sorting out values; of trying to reestablish reasonable priorities. We are wondering whether anything is worth our commitment or involvement, or whether we should withdraw and isolate ourselves. I'm afraid that, as a nation, we may opt for the latter, and turn our lives over to a ruling elite and quietly, even eagerly, accept a "benevolent dictatorship." We may give up our freedom, not because we are conquered by another nuclear power, or because our educators and our communications media brainwash us, but because we are just tired and confused, and we don't care anymore. We could each conclude that everything is absurd and drift off into our little dream worlds, as seemed to be the case in the movie *Blow Up,* which ended with two men playing an imaginary game of tennis, with imaginary rackets and balls, and then one of the players chasing off into the distance after the imaginary tennis ball as "the end" title came on the screen.

I doubt if we're going to realize some of the dire predictions, such as the earth disappearing into a black hole some-

day, or everybody dying of starvation because of overpopu-
lation, or everyone strangling from smog. I don't think any
of these physical problems is insurmountable. Life-styles
may have to change considerably, perhaps drastically, but
we'll find ways to solve the physical problems.

The real problems, as I see them, are the ones that deal
with morality and human behavior. And of all the things
we've lost and need to find again, I think the most important
is faith. Because we lost faith in our political leaders, in the
"system," in education, in the authenticity of sports, in ad-
vertising, in business, in preachers, in ourselves, and in a certain sense we lost faith in faith. Losing faith in faith may
sound like mere rhetoric, but I don't believe it is. I thought
it was significant that in summing up his comprehensive survey of American attitudes in 1973, pollster Louis Harris said
in a television interview, "People have lost confidence, but
not faith." Abraham Lincoln spoke of being "destitute of
faith but terrified of skepticism." It is extremely important,
in my opinion, that we maintain some grounds for faith in
something. I think it's important that we have faith in the
right things, but just faith itself can be the slender thread that
separates us from despair. Human beings have to believe in
something. The capacity to believe is essential, and in the
past decade or so, many have come close to losing it. As a
member of the White House press corps, I am in one of the
most skeptical groups of individuals in the world. But, in a
way, it's healthy to be skeptical. It's when skepticism turns
to cynicism that we have a very unhealthy condition. Someone said "cynicism is history half-learned." So I think cynicism, even now, is not justified. And somehow, out of the
sham and the phony and the hypocritical, we must cling to
faith in what is true. I mean, we've got to find and cherish
the moral reference point that will stand all tests. I don't
think it's farfetched to suggest that. If we need a worldwide

time signal as a reference in syncronizing our clocks, why doesn't it make sense that we need a reference point for what is true? What can the standard be then? Your conscience? My conscience? The law? We will repeat a bad mistake, we will not have learned the lesson of past experiences, if we look for our "North Star" among the glittering lights of human creation. If recent history has taught us anything, it is that the "lights" can fail—that our leaders have been fallible and corruptible. I don't know that I would go as far as the Russian anarchist Michael Bakunin, who said, "It is absolutely impossible for a man who wields power to remain a moral man," but Malcolm Muggeridge's conclusion is worth pondering: "The world always has been, and always will be, ruled by immoral men." It is essential to face up to man's limitations. There is an intriguing piece of sculpture in the Brookgreen Gardens, near Myrtle Beach, South Carolina, which depicts a man carving out his own form from stone. Obviously he can't complete it, because he can't even reach his back with the hammer and chisel. Man needs help! But having said that, it is important to realize that, with help, man is capable of fantastic accomplishments. Despite what I have said previously about the cussedness of man, he is not all bad, as some have concluded. He has great potential. He has mitigating qualities, and is capable of being decent, basically honest, compassionate, loving, honorable, fair, responsible. We all have a choice of whether to follow our bad or good instincts, and the hope of a worthwhile future for mankind lies in that choice. Hope for society lies in large measure in whether people follow the path of truth —whether they stick to what is true. To put it another way, much depends on what authentic people who have a grasp of what is true do. Will they be complacent? Isolated? Uninvolved? Sometime, somewhere, good people with high ideals are going to have to act on their assumptions. There has been too much of a tendency for people of high ideals to withdraw from the so-called "dirty" business of politics, the press, entertainment, and other worldly professions, into safe enclaves away from the real world; there to talk to themselves and cluck their tongues about how corrupt the world is becoming. Our society is in its present condition not because of what people of low morals did, but because of what people of high morality did not do. In his much-discussed book *The Gulag Archipelago, 1918-1956,* Alexander I. Solzhenitsyn observed that Stalin's machine would have ground to a halt if the people had resisted the mass arrests. "We lacked enough love of freedom," he said. And he declared that "after one unrestrained outburst in 1917, we made haste to be submissive. We submitted with pleasure."

We face a rare opportunity. The time may be right for new leadership—in politics, in education, in neighborhoods, and in all places of influence. Watergate, the turmoil of the '60's, the energy crisis, the environment problem, even the loss of confidence and direction, have put most people in the mood for change. The obvious example is politics. Until now, perhaps, it has been difficult for a person to get elected unless he sold himself to special interests, or bartered his integrity to party bosses. But now, maybe, voters will support and campaign for candidates of better quality. They may be more conscious of issues than of image. One of the better recruiting slogans has been: "The Marines are looking for a few good men." The world is looking for a few good men and women. If they respond, there is hope.

I would like to wrap up my thoughts with definite answers to all of the questions I have raised, both in regard to individuals and to our society. I would like to be able to suggest a simple cure for the loss of confidence. I would like to be able to prescribe the remedy for the sins of the press. I would like to articulate a surefire way to produce leaders with integrity and a way for the rest of us to recognize them. I would like to be able to point the way out of the confusion mankind has gotten lost in so that everyone would accept it and act on it.

It would be simple to say, "Love is the answer"; or "Awareness is the answer"; or even "God is the answer." In the context of what I have had to say up to this point, I could conclude that "Truth is the answer." All of these statements are valid, but only if implemented. You don't go riding through the streets announcing our troubles are over because of the great discovery, "Truth is the answer," and expect the world to be different the next day. So, to be practical, we must accept people as they are and as they are likely to continue to be, accepting the proposition that most can be improved. It is presumptious of me to offer an instant analysis, and I find that much easier than offering answers. Therefore, I have tried not to presume further by claiming there is a shortcut to restoration of confidence. Rather, I have tried to suggest a starting place for a long journey.